Rocks, Relics and Biblical Reliability

About the Author and Respondent

CLIFFORD A. WILSON

Clifford Wilson obtained his M.S. in archaeology from Sydney University in Australia, his B.D. from Melbourne College of Divinity, and his Ph.D. in psycholinguistics from the University of South Carolina.

He served for some years as Director of the Australian Institute of Archaeology. In addition to inspecting many of the Mideastern archaeological sites, in 1969 he served as area supervisor at the excavation of Gezer in Israel.

In 1971, Dr. Wilson was honored as an "outstanding educator in America." Currently, he is a senior lecturer at Monash University in Melbourne, Australia.

He is in demand in Australia, the United States, and Canada as a lecturer and is the author of several books, including *Crash Go the Chariots* (an archaeologist's reply to Von Daniken's *Chariots of the Gods*) and *That Incredible Book — the Bible*. In addition, he serves as consulting editor of *Bible and Spade,* a quarterly digest of biblical archaeology.

R. K. HARRISON

R. K. Harrison is professor of Old Testament at Wycliffe College at the University of Toronto. He is also a faculty member of the Toronto School of Theology. He holds a B.D., M.Th., and a Ph.D. from the University of London and has received an honorary D.D. from Huron College at the University of Western Ontario.

He is the author or the coauthor of a dozen books. Three of these books are devoted to archaeological topics: *The Dead Sea Scrolls, Archaeology of the Old Testament,* and *Archaeology of the New Testament.* His most recent works are *Old Testament Times* and *Introduction to the Old Testament*. He is also the editor of *The New International Commentary on the Old Testament.*

Rocks, Relics and Biblical Reliability

Clifford A. Wilson

with a response by
R. K. Harrison

ZONDERVAN PUBLISHING HOUSE
OF THE ZONDERVAN CORPORATION
GRAND RAPIDS, MICHIGAN 49506

PROBE MINISTRIES
INTERNATIONAL
RICHARDSON, TEXAS 75080

Copyright   © 1977 by Probe Ministries International

Library of   Wilson, Clifford A
Congress   Rocks, relics, and Biblical reliability.
Cataloging in
Publication Data   (Christian free university curriculum)
                    Bibliography: p.
                    1.   Bible—Antiquities.   I.   Title.   II.   Series.
                 BS621.W466   220.1   77-9415

ISBN   0-310-35701-2

Place of
Printing   *Printed in the United States of America*

Permissions   Macmillan Publishing Company (15); British Museum (17,22,
                  89,92,96,99); University Museum of the University of Pennsylvania
                  (30); Religious News Service [top] and World Wide Photos [bottom]
                  (33); Matson Photo Service (36,71); Oriental Institute of the Univer-
                  sity of Chicago (40,51); American Schools of Oriental Research
                  (43,107); Brooklyn Museum (48); Van Elderen (61); Levant (64);
                  Busby (80,113); Historical Picture Service (118)

Design   Cover design by Paul Lewis
            Book design by Louise Bauer

What is Probe?

Probe Ministries is a nonprofit corporation organized to provide perspective on the integration of the academic disciplines and historic Christianity. The members and associates of the Probe team are actively engaged in research as well as lecturing and interacting in thousands of university classrooms throughout the United States and Canada on topics and issues vital to the university student.

Christian Free University books should be ordered from Zondervan Publishing House (in the United Kingdom from The Paternoster Press), but further information about Probe's materials and ministries may be obtained by writing to Probe Ministries International, Box 5012, Richardson, Texas 75080.

Contents

Illustrations

Book Abstract

The basic question considered is: Can the biblical documents be regarded as historically reliable? The past century has been extremely rich in archaeological research of ancient Israel and her neighbors in the Near East. Much information has come to light touching on biblical history, both validating and enlarging the view of life in the ancient world as pictured in the Bible. This survey examines, period by period, highlights from the interlacings of secular and biblical history and the reliability of the documents of the Old and New Testaments in light of these findings.

chapter one

What Biblical Archaeology Is All About

The archaeologist's purpose of reconstructing the past bears incidentally but significantly on the question of the historical accuracy of the biblical documents. Each of the tools, procedures, and common kinds of discoveries of this maturing science are viewed.

Grandma says the Bible is "God's Word" and she doesn't care what anybody says. Granddad says all these "other" translations are what's causing problems—"shouldn't read anything but the King James." Mom says living a good life is what is really important, and Dad says just be careful what and whom you believe, and don't be a fanatic either way—believing or disbelieving.

At the university the biologist claims the Bible is full of holes when considered scientifically. The historian says there are problems in dating and accuracy; the book has been recopied and translated so many times nobody knows what it originally said. The English professor admires it, but only for its poetry and sym-   11 bolism. And the philosopher thinks mankind has finally graduated from former primitive religious myths and now can face his cosmos unafraid. Man no longer needs security-blanket explanations from "sacred writings" concerning the nature of reality and the universe. He can discern meaning and values within himself.

There are many opinions today about the Bible and its worth to students, parents, educators, and even religious leaders. The questions can be approached in a variety of ways and from different disciplines. The purpose of this book is to consider the evidence as seen in archaeology for or against the reliability of the Bible and to suggest conclusions supported by that evidence.

Let it be immediately said that we do not suggest that archaeology "proves" the Bible. The Bible is primarily a book of spiritual assertions, and as such its "proof" is beyond history. But even in matters of history, the Bible touches on many thousands of incidents, facts, and people, and to suggest that archaeology "proves" the Bible's history would be a sweeping generalization. It is also true that there are areas of problem where it is not easy to reconcile biblical data with the accepted results of archaeology. Such areas are few and far between and they have a strange habit of disappearing as further results come to hand. There is in fact no actual area where it can be said that here the original manuscripts of the Bible are in error, as proved conclusively by archaeological research.

Nor are we begging the question by referring to "the original manuscripts." Such a stand must necessarily be taken. We simply do not have the original manuscripts of the Bible, and it is good that we do not. Because mankind is constantly idolizing religious relics, doubtless the manuscripts of the Bible would be worshiped if they were in existence. The noteworthy thing is that the copies we have are remarkably preserved and amazingly accurate. Some problems with our texts arise from the natural limitations of the language. Some Hebrew letters of the alphabet were also used as numbers and there were no vowels. Considering the similarity of some of the letters, occasional errors in numbers and word meanings are not surprising. Context becomes very important in deciding a particular meaning. However, the amazing accuracy of the texts used in translation can be illustrated by the findings from the Dead Sea Scrolls. While minor improvements of the texts have been necessary, not one single doctrine of the Bible has been altered following the discovery of these scrolls.

Another cautionary note should be stated at the beginning of this survey. Many people think that the main purpose of archaeologists is to find evidence to support the Bible. That is simply not true. Archaeologists are scholars, usually having little interest in the Bible, except as another historical book that might occasionally touch on their own excavations. Where that does happen, they are delighted, for it gives them a reliable dating point and helps them to set surrounding facts in proper focus.

I was an area supervisor at the excavation of Gezer in 1969.* We found a huge layer of ash, sometimes as deep as three feet. It ran for a considerable distance across the tell (mound), and when we carefully sieved in the surrounding areas, we found artifacts showing that Hebrew, Philistine, and Egyptian cultures had met at that point of time. Other evidence suggested that we were excavating material from the time period associated with Solomon. When the leaders discussed the whole of the findings, they realized that the Bible had something to say at this point. They consulted 1 Kings 9:16ff., where it is stated quite clearly that the Egyptian Pharaoh conquered the Philistines at Gezer and gave the city to Solomon when Solomon married the Pharaoh's daughter.

At that time, so the Bible states, the city was thoroughly burned by fire. We as excavators had come across the evidence of that destruction. The leaders, including G. Ernest Wright of Harvard and Nelson Glueck of the Hebrew Union College, were delighted,

---

*The Gezer excavation was undertaken by the American Schools of Oriental Research in association with the Hebrew Union College in Jerusalem.

not because we had "proved the Bible" but because we had come across a highly relevant dating point that was of great value in this academic exercise.

That incident highlights the change in approach that has come to characterize the work of biblical archaeology. It is true that few archaeologists set out to "prove" the Bible, but it is also true that in the last forty years a tremendous change of attitude toward the Bible has emerged. No longer is it thought that the Bible is more likely to be wrong than right, but it has become respectable to recognize the Bible as a reliable source book. It is openly studied, and those who know their facts regard it as a first-class history textbook. As G. E. Wright says concerning earlier views that the Bible was little more than myth or legend, "For the most part archaeology has substantiated and illumined the biblical story at so many crucial points that no one can seriously take this position."[1]

A Maturing Science

The word *archaeology* itself comes from two Greek words—*arche,* which means "beginning," and *logos,* which means "word." Archaeology is concerned with the study of beginnings and is traditionally associated with the study of settled remains of human civilization. Another discipline, anthropology, deals with early man, as distinct from man's settled civilizations. The material remains of a culture are studied by archaeologists so that the culture of the times can be recaptured and the background built up.[2] Palaces, temples, libraries, workshops, ornaments, bas-reliefs, pottery, tools, and writing materials of various shapes, sizes, and texture, are all important for the archaeologist as he works with his pick, his *pateche* (hand pick), his sieve, and his trowel. Cemeteries and tombs are important, but so also are hiding places — as witness the famous Dead Sea Scrolls, which were found in almost inaccessible caves alongside the Dead Sea in 1947 and the years following.

Natural calamities, such as that associated with the destruction of the Roman cities of Pompeii and Herculaneum, have sometimes sealed off civilizations at a particular point of time. They have often preserved information about the people who once occupied the region. Pottery and other household goods and various types of traded objects are all relevant in the dating and reconstruction of a particular time period.

Often the ancient sites are located at what is known as a *tell*, this being an Arabic word that literally means "hill." These are artificial hills that have accumulated over a period of time. A site might be occupied for a short time and then become deserted, perhaps because of fire, earthquake, ravages of war, or infectious disease, or perhaps even because the trade route has changed. Time goes by, and the advantages of the site are again recognized, and so newcomers level off the debris of the old city and build again. Sometimes old buildings are reconstructed, but at other times they are completely destroyed. Thus a tell grows, level by level, much like a big layer cake; and when modern archaeologists excavate, it is usual to go down in a selected area, level by level, starting from the most recent times and working down toward bedrock, to the time when the site was first occupied. At the present time, only a small fraction of the once-occupied tells in Bible lands have been excavated.[3]

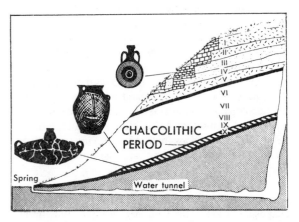

Schematic section of a tell

One great difference between Israel and her neighbors is that, in the main, Israel's history has not needed to be uncovered. Her history has been preserved in the

Old Testament, and it has been remarkable to find how accurately that history has been recorded. Thus, while it is true that archaeology does not set out to "prove" the Bible, it is also true that archaeology has confirmed the historical value of the Bible at many points.

Archaeology is no longer a haphazard exercise. Scholars simply cannot go off and dig wherever they like. Local ownership and government regulations prevent that, and, in any case, excavation is a costly and time-consuming activity. While many discoveries have been made by random exploration, most excavations now proceed methodically. Interest is often triggered by information gleaned from a study of potsherds (pieces of broken pottery) found lying on a tell, the discovery of an exposed section of a building— perhaps after heavy rainfall—or even new geographical information arising from nearby sources. Other factors may precipitate interest as well. Perhaps the ancient name of a site is found to be surprisingly close to the name recorded in the Bible, or knowledge of an ancient fortress or trade route may single out an area. When sufficient interest has been generated, often a preliminary survey can serve to confirm expectations for a site.

Treasure is often found, although that is not the major objective of archaeological excavation. Pottery, tools, weapons, and objects associated with worship or with commerce — such as seals, weights, and coins — are all relevant. Inscriptions and other literary records are highly prized, and as items such as these are found, they are carefully recorded and often photographed. Archaeology is a true science, and anyone who has worked on a modern excavation with accepted academic leadership is aware that painstaking procedures, including careful recording, are insisted upon.

Important Finds

Inscriptions and written materials come in many shapes and sizes. There are large upright stone monuments known as *steles,* one of the best known to Bible students being the stele of Pharaoh (Merneptah).[4] This dates to about 1220 B.C. and refers to the desolation of Israel at that time. Another is the famous Moabite

Stone, which tells of the rebellion of King Mesha, an event also recorded in the Bible in 2 Kings 3.[5] The Black Obelisk of Shalmaneser shows King Jehu of Israel (or his emissary) prostrate and paying tribute before the Assyrian king Shalmaneser III.[6] Omri and

Black Obelisk of Shalmaneser III with top panels showing Jehu bringing tribute.

Shalmaneser are both known in the Bible, but this particular incident is not. Sometimes archaeology adds to our knowledge of Bible incidents and people, as in this instance.

Broken pottery was often used as a means of communication, and pottery inscribed with writing is known as *ostraca*. Important examples that are relevant to Bible history are the Samaria Ostraca,[7] dating to the time of the Israelite King Jeroboam II, and the Lachish Ostraca,[8] dating to the time of Nebuchadnezzar's campaigns against the cities of Judah, just before Jerusalem fell.

Parchment (animal skin), which was an important writing material, is sometimes found. Many of the Dead Sea Scrolls were written on parchment. Papyrus (a broad, flat leaf that in early times grew in the Nile Valley) was used to a great extent in Egypt, and the famous discoveries at the turn of this century by Grenfell, Hunt, and Hogarth were written on papyrus. Those findings did a great deal to show that the New Testament documents were written in the everyday Greek of New Testament times.[9]

Bas-reliefs (sculpturing projected slightly forward from background) and inscriptions on the walls of palaces, scarabs (images of a beetle deity, ranging from one to ten centimeters) showing the names of kings and important officials, cylinder seals telling of military conquests and other historical events, and, of course, thousands of clay tablets inscribed with cuneiform, have all been tremendously important as the history of Israel's neighbors has been reconstructed. Even jar handles inscribed with the names of a manufacturer have been very helpful—as with the handles that aided in the identification of El Jib, the ancient biblical city of Gibeon.[10]

Jewelry and cosmetics, mirrors and statuettes, ivory ornaments and children's toys, sewing needles with eyes, spindles, grinding and mill stones, dye vats, potters' kilns, and wine vats all point to various aspects of ancient culture and help to fill out the picture of Israel's neighbors and at times of the Hebrews themselves.

History in the Early Chapters of Genesis

The biblical stories of Creation, the Flood, and the Tower of Babel are shown to have primacy over parallel epics of the Ancient Near East. Historical corroboration of the Table of Nations and the recent Ebla finds further support the reliability of early Genesis.

The first eleven chapters of the Book of Genesis can be viewed in a number of ways. They are sometimes referred to as ''The Seed Plot of the Bible,'' for in them some of the major doctrines are presented for the first time. God is seen as the omnipotent Creator, the One who brought the heavens and the earth into being at His word. He is the great Revealer who communicated with Adam, the crown of His creation. He is pictured there as the holy God who must punish sin, even though it means driving man from the paradise prepared for him and later bringing the judgment of a great flood upon the earth. He is the merciful God who will   19 give man every opportunity of repenting from his sins. He is the redeemer God, for at the time of the Flood He made it possible for the righteous man Noah and his family to escape in a great ship. The character of God that is seen in Genesis 1–11 is presented consistently throughout the Bible, in both the Old and New Testaments.

The first eleven chapters also can be regarded as a necessary historical background to Abraham who appears, as on a stage, toward the end of chapter 11. The Old Testament is a survey of Israel's history, with Abraham as the father of the nation. As history, Genesis 1–11 is a brief introduction, showing the line through which Abraham descended.

In modern times there is still a tendency among many scholars to dismiss these first eleven chapters as mythological or at best legendary. They are supposedly stories to explain the beginning of mankind, the sorrow of motherhood, and the riddles associated with the creation of the world. Some scholars argue that a talking serpent cannot be accepted as historical fact and that there is no place today where cherubim are located with swords drawn to block entry to a hallowed place. They argue that trees cannot bear the "knowledge of good and evil," for these are immaterial qualities.

Such matters are outside the realm of historical "proof," but that is not to suggest that they are nonhistorical. The fact that something is not happening today does not mean that it has never happened. If there is a God, the miraculous is entirely acceptable, and many things that are not happening every day of every year could indeed have happened at appointed moments of time. Let it be clearly stated, however, that the events of Genesis 1–11 involve the miraculous, but not the magical. There is an essential difference between the miraculous and the magical, as we can see when we compare the early biblical records with those from Babylonia and Assyria.[11]

Parallels to Genesis

Certainly, archaeology cannot "prove" everything associated with Genesis 1–11, but there are some surprising indications that the records must be taken seriously.

In the Bible itself the Garden of Eden is described in straightforward terms and is even given a geographic location involving known rivers of ancient times. In the New Testament, the Epistle to the Romans builds an important theological argument around the concept of a literal man, Adam. While we cannot say exactly where the Garden of Eden was, we can look at Genesis 2:13,14 and see references to such places as Ethiopia, Assyria, and the Tigris (Hiddekel) and Euphrates rivers. Thus the general area is known and the Bible clues suggest it was much more extensive than just a "garden" as we think of one today.

Other ancient peoples also referred to some land that was traditionally in the general area of the Persian Gulf, one early record being the *Epic of Emmerkar*, which gives details about the land known as Dilmun.[12] We are told that birth in that land was without distress until Enki ate certain plants that involved a deadly curse. The Epic tells us that the land was a clear and pure place, that the lion did not kill, and that the lamb and the lion lived together peacefully. There was no sickness, and mankind had only one speech by which he addressed the gods. The recently recovered Ebla tablets refer to Dilmun, and this indicates that this place is a historical site. Thus it is probable that the *Epic of Emmerkar* is based on fact and is not merely a legendary tale.

There are other early stories of Creation and the Flood; and although they have become corrupted and distorted, they tell of gods creating heaven and earth, of man coming directly from the gods, and of man being immediately intelligent and civilized. Then man offended the gods; he was expelled from his garden paradise, and misery and sorrow followed.[13]

The Babylonian epic *Enuma Elish* tells of Creation; the *Epic of Gilgamesh* includes the story of the Flood; and the more recently recovered *Epic of Atrahasis* brings both Creation and Flood together in a continuing story. These have some surface similarities to the Bible records, but in the Bible we do not read of gods fighting, cutting each other in half, making the River Euphrates flow through one eye and the River Tigris through the other; nor do we read of man being created from the blood of an evil god, mixed with clay. Clearly, those Babylonian records have become corrupted, conveying grotesque concepts of deity that are quite foreign to the records of the Bible.[14]

A clay tablet of the Gilgamesh Epic inscribed in cuneiform and relating the Babylonian flood story.

Despite the polytheism in those Sumerian, Babylonian, and Assyrian records (the Assyrians copied from the earlier writings), the clay tablets have enough similarity to the records in Genesis to merit serious consideration of how and why they are related. Today archaeologists recognize that legends and traditions are usually based on fact. Homer's *Atlantis* is no longer seen as the poetic license of a great dreamer, but rather it is now accepted as fact that there was an original Atlantis. So it is with these records of Creation and the Flood: many scholars agree it is reasonable to assume that the narrative of Genesis 1–11 is far more factual than their counterparts would have conceded in the previous generation. They do not agree as to where the figurative and the literal merge in Bible history, and some would insist on symbolic interpretation, while others are more definite regarding literal meaning. Nevertheless, the actual historical basis for these Bible records is not challenged to the extent that it was a generation ago.

Another recently translated creation account is the *Epic of Atrahasis,* of which about four-fifths has been restored from a copy dating to about 1630 B.C. Fragments of it have been found at a number of ancient sites, including Nineveh, Babylon, Nippur, and Baghozkoy. In this epic, the Flood story is also included, and there are points of comparison and contrasts with the Bible records, as there are with *Enuma Elish* and the *Epic of Gilgamesh.* Again, the superiority of the Bible record becomes clear as the records are compared.[15]

The Primacy of Genesis

One scholar who analyzes the evidence is A. R. Millard. He touches on another highly relevant point with regard to the Bible record. He concludes his survey on this new "Babylonian Genesis" story as follows:

> All who suspect or suggest borrowing by the Hebrews are compelled to admit large-scale revision, alteration, and reinterpretation in a fashion which cannot be substantiated for any other composition from the ancient Near East or in any other Hebrew writing. . . . Careful comparison of ancient texts and literary methods is the only way to the understanding of the early chapters of Genesis. Discovery of new material requires reassessment of former conclusions; so the Epic of Atrahasis adds to knowledge of parallel Babylonian traditions, and of their literary form. All speculation apart, it underlines the uniqueness of the Hebrew primaeval history in the form in which it now exists.[16]

The Bible record does not include polytheism or crude mythology, or amoral activity that is absurdly grotesque, as in the Babylonian epics. Kenneth A. Kitchen of the University of Liverpool has another noteworthy comment:

> The common assumption that the Hebrew account is simply a purged and simplified version of the Babylonian legend (applied also to the Flood stories) is fallacious on methodological grounds. In the Ancient Near East, the rule is that simple accounts or traditions may give rise (by

accretion and embellishment) to elaborate legends, but not vice versa. In the ancient Orient, legends were not simplified or turned into pseudo-history (historicized) as has been assumed for early Genesis.[17]

Part of the *Epic of Gilgamesh* has been found in excavations at Megiddo in ancient Palestine (now Israel). This fragment predates by about a thousand years the copy recovered last century from the palace of the great Assyrian king Ashurbanipal. This discovery indicated that the story was widely known throughout the "Fertile Crescent"—that great fertile area stretching up through modern Iraq, down through Israel, and across into Egypt. This finding also indicated that this record had actually been carried across much of that strip of land relatively close to the times of the patriarchs (Abraham, Isaac, and Jacob). This being the case, it is conceivable that the early records of Genesis likewise have been carried across the Fertile Crescent, probably even by Abraham himself. There are clues within the Bible records to suggest that the clay tablets were handed over at the time of the death of the "clan leader," and that the one who took over the tablets at that time was responsible for bringing them up to date. The late P. J. Wiseman suggested a convincing argument that the early chapters of Genesis were originally on clay tablets. He put forward the idea of a colophon (a connecting link between clay tablets) showing that these early records of Genesis were actually put down in writing. He argued that the literary aids demonstrated in Genesis indicate "that the Book was compiled at an early date, certainly not later than the age of Moses."

Wiseman suggests that the repetition of words and phrases points to different clay tablets, the first words of the new tablet being a repetition of the last words of the previous record. He argues that this can be seen as follows:

Genesis 1:1: "God created the heavens and the earth" (cf. 2:4);
Genesis 2:4: "when they were created" (cf. 5:2);

Genesis 6:10: "Shem, Ham, and Japheth" (cf. 10:1);
Genesis 10:1: "after the Flood" (cf. 11:10);
Genesis 11:26: "Abram, Nahor, and Haran" (cf. 11:27);
Genesis 25:12: "Abraham's son" (cf. 25:19);
Genesis 36:1: "Who is Edom" (cf. 36:8);
Genesis 36:9: "father of the Edomites" (literally, "Father Edom"—cf. 36:43).

He adds elaborate evidence to show similar practices from the written records of the ancient East, his point being that these early Bible records follow the recognized pattern.[18]

It is entirely possible that these clay tablets were passed on through the first-born son of the succeeding families until they came into possession of the family of Moses. He was then responsible to compile them into the record we now know as Genesis.

There are other aspects of Genesis 1–11 that are challenged by modern critics. We read of long-living men, such as Methuselah, who outlived all others by attaining the great age of 969 years. This biblical material has long embarrassed its adherents and scandalized the skeptics. Various attempts to explain it have been made. For example, it has been suggested that months, not years, are the time spans totaled there. However, to suggest that the years were of shorter duration—such as months—does not solve the problems. For instance, we read that Seth became a father at 105, Enoch at 90, and Kenan at 70. If a year was only a month, these men became fathers at ages ranging between six and ten years of age, and that is obviously ruled out. We do not know that these were the ages when they first became fathers, but that at that particular time each became the father of a specific son.

There is much that we do not understand, and obviously there are factors that are outside present historical occurrence, but this dissimilarity to our context is no basis to rule them out.

The Problem of Longevity

Prior to rejecting this information, the careful historian is intrigued by the provocative parallel accounts of other peoples. The Greek historian Berossus, for example, listed the ten kings of Babylon who lived "before the Flood," and he gave their reigns as varying from 10,800 years to 64,800 years, with an overall total of 432,000 years. Clearly, those ages are unacceptable as life spans, or even as lengths of dynasties, but they do suggest that there is a basis for the belief that men lived for considerably longer periods of time in the remote past. That tradition is known to many ancient peoples, including the Egyptians, the Chinese, the Greeks, and the Romans.

It is entirely possible that the ages of people might well have been calculated according to some scheme that was familiar in antiquity but is now unknown to us. There is also a symbolic use of numbers, and Bible students recognize that numbers such as seven and forty had special significance to the Jewish people. Possibly the age of Joseph at his death is in this category, for "110 years of age" was the Egyptian way of saying that a man was "full of years"—that he had lived a full life that was rich in accomplishments and of great benefit to others. It is possible that in some way unknown to us, the large numbers given to the lives of these early Genesis people also have some symbolic significance. It is likely, however, that the figures do have a factual basis. Genesis 1–11 is an area of Scripture that consistently turns out to be historical after all.

Although we reject figures like those of Berossus, it is entirely possible that men might have lived for hundreds of years. We do not know how man's physical well-being has been affected by climatic changes, disease, diet, and even the social problems of developing civilizations. Gerontologists are beginning to state that ages much longer than our present life spans are entirely possible for man, and researchers are talking about a major breakthrough.[19] For example, one theory of aging is known as the cross-linkage theory. If cross-linkage is the cause of aging, it is possible that enzymes or other means may be found to break down this process, virtually removing the aging mechanism.

Could it be that such an enzyme occurred naturally in man until changes in climate or radiation intensity eliminated it from his genetic code?

A Change of Atmosphere?

Another relevant point is that the Genesis record shows that man lived for a considerably shorter period of time after the Flood. It seems probable that atmospheric changes of far-reaching importance took place at that time. Genesis 2:5,6 tells us that prior to this time the earth had been watered by a mist coming up from the earth, and this is a statement now taken seriously. Later, different atmospheric conditions prevailed on the earth, with ultraviolet rays being active with a greater intensity, probably leading to the production of cancer and other new developments on the earth.

There are various indications of climatic changes that fit the biblical picture, such as the remains of tropical growth found beneath the ice at the South Pole, and similar evidence of luxurious growth found in the stomachs of animals that had suddenly been encased in ice in Siberia. A catastrophe such as the Flood could have caused these fantastic changes in vegetation in relatively recent times.

Climatic changes, the dating of early man, and anthropology are really only of fringe interest in our specialty of biblical archaeology. At the same time, it is relevant at least to touch on the subject. One point is clear: the Bible dates are not as suspect as seemed possible a generation ago.[20]

Possibly the changes in atmospheric conditions were associated with a water-vapor blanket around the earth until the time of the Flood. Such a theory is put forward seriously by competent men of science. Indeed, it is even put forward in one of the papers submitted in January 1970 to the Lunar Science conference at Houston, Texas. A. E. Ringwood reported that his investigation of lunar rock samples indicated that most of the accepted theories about the origin of the moon were wrong. Part of Ringwood's conclusion was that early in the earth's history it had a massive atmosphere, at a high-enough temperature to evaporate certain elements being collected by the earth's movement through space. Although he personally is not identifying this with the Flood, such a statement indicates that this idea of an atmospheric envelope should be taken seriously. It could explain long-living men, the shielding of our earth from dangerous ultraviolet and other rays, and the sudden death of animals in areas not tropical, but with large quantities of undigested tropical food in their stomachs. An atmospheric canopy might have given the world a uniform climate.[21]

In Genesis 1–11 we are dealing with some aspects that are supra-historical — they are beyond our present (and perhaps future) knowledge of history, but they should not be discarded as nonhistorical for that reason. Perhaps it is also relevant to state that when we compare the Bible's longevity figures with those of other accounts, such as the Sumerians', the Bible's figures are found to be conservative, and we gain the impression that those other records have grown in the telling.[22]

More Confirmed Information

One particular document in Genesis 1–11 is the so-called "Table of Nations" (Gen. 10). In addition to longevity figures, the Table of Nations involves linguistic, physical, and geographical features. Although some of the people mentioned in this table cannot be identified, few Bible readers realize that it is accepted today as being a remarkably accurate and informative document. The renowned William Foxwell Albright referred to it in his book *Recent Discoveries in Bible Lands* and suggested that it stands absolutely alone in ancient literature and is an astonishingly accurate document. He went on to say that scholars never fail to be impressed with the author's knowledge of the subject.[23]

Even the story of the Tower of Babel (Gen. 11) is no longer looked on as being without foundation. Not all scholars will accept it as a literal record, but there has been a considerable amount of evidence to suggest that at one time men did speak one language, and very possibly that various languages, with their later divergencies, had their origin in the general area of Sumer, the biblical Shinar.[24]

We do know that ancient peoples often built their cities around sacred towers, as illustrated at cities such as Ur and Kish in ancient Babylonia. In building the Tower of Babel, men were possibly thinking of being safe in case another flood judgment came; or perhaps they were setting themselves up as a super people, with their tower opposing the glory of a true God. In the pattern of ancient temple towers, the shrine of the god was placed at the top and became the focal point of worship and unholy practices. Albright suggests, "It was, therefore, as a tremendous monument to its builders that the Tower of Babel was intended."[25] Albright suggests that the word *sem* does not mean "name," but an inscribed monument. The biblical story says that man's rebellion and self-glorification had led once again to the judgment of God, not by a flood, but this time by a confusion of his language, and he was scattered throughout the earth.

It is interesting to note that Ur-Nammu, King of Ur from about 2044 to 2007 B.C., supposedly received orders to build a great ziggurat (temple tower) as an act of worship to the moon god Nannar. A stele (monument) about 5 feet across and 10 feet high shows Ur-Nammu's various activities, and one panel has him setting out with a mortar basket to begin construction of the great tower. In this way he was showing his allegiance to the gods by taking his place as a humble workman. A clay tablet has been unearthed that states that the erection of the tower offended the gods, so they threw down what men had built, scattered them abroad, and made their speech strange. This of course is remarkably similar to the record in the Bible.

In a series of essays dedicated to the memory of archaeologist E. A. Speiser, one paper was presented by S. N. Kramer of the University of Pennsylvania, entitled "The Babel of Tongues—A Sumerian Version." Kramer pointed out that Speiser had analyzed, with characteristic acumen, learning, and skill, the Mesopotamian background of the narrative relating to the Tower of Babel and had come to the conclusion that this narrative had a demonstrable

Rocks, Relics,
and Biblical
Reliability

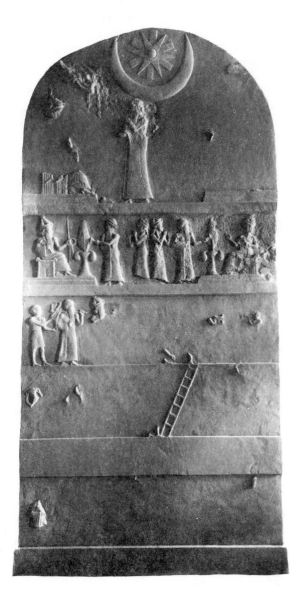

*Ur-Nammu stele
with the middle
panel showing the
king setting out to
begin construction
of a great tower for
the moon god Nan-
nar.*

source in cuneiform literature.[26] He went on to speak of a new parallel to the motif in the Tower of Babel record, relating to the confusion of tongues.[27]

Oxford cuneiformist Oliver Gurney is yet another who has contributed to this theme by his translation of a fragmentary tablet touching on a Sumerian version of the Babel story.[28] In that recovered record we learn that the whole universe was able to worship their god in unison, in one tongue.

As Kramer summarizes the evidence, he points out that the new tablet to which he has referred puts it beyond doubt that the Sumerians believed there was a time when all mankind spoke one and the same language and that the time came when the God of Wisdom confounded their speech.[29]

A Sensational Recent Finding

As we draw to the close of this chapter, one last highly significant recent find should be mentioned. Two Italian archaeologists, Paola Matthiae and Giovanni Pettinato of the University of Rome, have been working in Syria and have unearthed about seventeen thousand clay tablets at Tell Mardikh, believed to be the site of ancient Ebla.[30] This city was known from references in Sumerian, Akkadian, Hittite, and Egyptian texts, but before this excavation (the Italian team commenced excavating in 1964) there was doubt as to the location of the actual site.

Tell Mardikh is about thirty miles south of Aleppo and the recovered inscriptions indicate that this is apparently the actual site of Ebla. The tablets are a mixture of logograms (utilizing a symbol to represent a word or concept) and syllabic units that spell out words used by people of this area—these latter even give clues to vowel structures, and this alone is an exciting discovery for the linguist.

Some of the words so spelled out are *ab-ra-mu* (Abraham), *e-sa-um* (Esau), *da-'u-dum* (David), *sa-'u-lum* (Saul), *mi-ka-ilu* (Michael), and *is-ra-ilu* (Israel). These are not the biblical characters themselves, but the use of such names by people associated with the ancestor of Abraham is an indication that such biblical names were in use.

Another person is Ibrium, one of the kings of Ebla, and some discussion has centered around the possibility that he was the "Eber" referred to in Genesis 10 as the great-great-great-great-grandfather of the biblical Abraham. Both Abraham's name and that of the Hebrew people possibly have as their root this same Eber. It may not have been the same Eber, but the ethnic connection with the Hebrew makes it a distinct possibility.

In addition to other biblical associations, the tablets give accounts of the creation of the world and a great flood. The flood record is similar to the Babylonian accounts discussed earlier in this chapter, but the creation record is remarkably close to that of Genesis 1. This Eblaite tablet tells of the creation of the heavens, the earth, the sun, and the moon by one great being. The rest of the tablet has not yet been translated. Scholars at the time were astonished that what they considered a first-millennium oral Hebrew tradition was now found in a written third-millennium document. This is a clear pointer to the antiquity of the Genesis record, as well as that from Ebla.

The excavation continues. In fact, the seventeen thousand tablets found in 1975 and 1976 came from a miscellany of records kept near the central court area, and it is hoped that even more will be recovered as the main body of the palace is excavated. The chief tablet collection would normally be stored in the royal archive, and those recovered were not from this royal archive. If it is recovered, the findings will be even more sensational.

This level of the city's occupation dates to about 2300 B.C., and the references indicate that the Canaanite people controlled a major empire in that part of the world, between the 26th and 23rd centuries B.C. The tablets refer to various sites, including *urusalima* (Jerusalem), Hazor, Lachish, Megiddo, Gaza, Sinai, Joppa, and Haran. The five cities of the plain (Gen. 14:2), including Sodom and Gomorrah, are referred to, and so also is Salim, apparently the city of Melchizedek, who is also referred to in Genesis 14. The Canaanites are usually credited with the development of what became alphabetic writing, and there are many

*Some of the over
17,000 Eblaite tab-
lets discovered at
Tell-Mardikh.*

*A double basin
from Tell-Mardikh
with engravings
of lambs and
royal figures.*

close parallels between the language of these tablets and ancient Hebrew. Included in the finds was a bilingual vocabulary list that contained approximately one thousand words in both Sumerian logograms and Ebla's syllabic form of writing. This correlation is of great importance for the purposes of translation of the tablets.

David Noel Freedman of the University of Michigan traveled to Rome especially to interview the Italian archaeologists. In a widely reported prepared statement, he announced, "Previous reports and rumors do not begin to indicate the true dimensions of the discovery and its importance for ancient Near Eastern and Biblical studies. . . . A new chapter in the history of the Near East has been opened and it will not be closed for some time. . . ." He further stated, "Should the royal archive be found intact, there is no way to calculate either the size or the importance of such a collection, but in view of what has turned up in an adjunct repository, the possibilities stagger the imagination."[31]

This material could be elaborated on considerably as in the term *Ya* (later an abbreviated form of *Yahweh*) in personal names. One result from Ebla is that the early chapters of Genesis touched by the findings are again seen as remarkably credible.

The fact is, many seemingly mythological records must be taken seriously after all. As we compare the biblical with the nonbiblical accounts, we find that these records of early Genesis are far more acceptable than seemed possible a century ago. Tablet after tablet has been recovered, and we are able to see similarities to many Bible documents. It is significant, too, that the Bible records have a habit of proving superior to the distorted and often grotesque records of the same events as they are known from the libraries of Israel's neighbors.

chapter three

The Roots of a Nation

Beginning with Woolley's excavation of Ur, the excavation of most of the cities associated with Abraham has shown the intimate interplay between biblical and secular history. Biblical stories such as those of Abraham's purchase of the cave of Machpelah and Esau's sale of his birthright are enriched by the revealing of archaeology's secrets.

At one time some scholars contended that the patriarchal records of Genesis (purportedly of 2000 B.C.) were really reflections of the time of the divided kingdom after Solomon (975 B.C.) and not of the times of Abraham and his immediate descendants a thousand years earlier. This view, of course, denied the historicity of the entire patriarchal records.

No people live in complete isolation, and as we study Bible history, we necessarily glance at other peoples in the ancient Near East. In this way, the story of Abraham and his descendants can be filled out or negated. First, we find Abraham living in lower Mesopotamia, probably near the city of Ur. Almost certainly he did not live in the city itself, for he was a   35 trader and moved around with sheep, cattle, and camels. He probably visited the city from time to time to buy and sell. Earlier suggestions that the references to camels are anachronisms (persons or things that are chronologically out of place) are now ruled out. Figurines of kneeling camels date back to hundreds of years before the time of Abraham and, though they did not come into great domestic use until after the time of Abraham, there were many camels being used by traders in his day.[32]

The city identified by Sir Leonard Woolley as Ur was an impressive center as early as 2700 B.C., and its royal tombs or death pits demonstrate the remarkable culture that had been achieved in this area hundreds of years before the time of Abraham. This finding threw great light on patriarchal backgrounds and the ancient Sumerian civilization. Woolley recovered a golden helmet, golden drinking vessels, jewelry and ornaments of gold and silver, a plumbing system of clay pipes running out of some houses, musical instruments with up to thirteen strings, and even two-storied houses having as many as fourteen rooms. Evidences showed that the richer people were able to send their sons to school, where they studied cube roots and even a crude form of what we know as the Pythagorean Theorem.

Excavation at Ur, which revealed a sophisticated culture earlier than Abraham's time.

Woolley's Pelican book *Ur of the Chaldees* still sells after a quarter of a century. The biblical clarification "of the Chaldees" is an indication that the Bible writer knew of another Ur, and the Ebla texts tell of such a city to the north, in the territory of Haran. The fact that later writers also refer to "Ur of the Chaldees" (e.g., Neh. 9:7) indicates that it was indeed the southern city. Woolley's identification of "his" city with Abraham was correct.

The Bible: Witness of the Times

The findings at Eshnunna, a few miles out of modern Baghdad, included the famous code of laws of King Bilalama, dating to about 250 years before Hammurabi.[33] Another code of laws was that of Lipit-Ishtar, the fifth ruler of Isin, who left a code on seven clay tablets, dating to about 1860 B.C.[34] The well-known Hammurabi codified laws were established in his own time (about 1700 B.C.). These findings indicate that law codes were relatively common before Abraham's time. The recent findings at Ebla (the modern Tell Mardikh in Syria) indicate that substantial law codes were known in that period of civilization, about 2300 B.C.[35] There are indications of the submission of biblical figures to such codes in the Bible records. One good example is Abraham's reluctance to send the girl Hagar away, for we now know that the law of his day made it clear that he had responsibilities toward her. Not until he was given a higher revelation from God was he prepared to allow her to depart from the protection of his household.[36]

From other cities with occupation dating to about the time of Abraham, we find that various Bible names were then known. They are usually not referring to the biblical figures bearing the same names, but they do indicate that the names were correctly used. Thus, at Mari on the River Euphrates letters using such names as Jacob-el, Abam-Ram (Abraham), and "Benjamites" have been recovered.[37] In Genesis 14 there is a record of five kings fighting against four kings, and the names there recorded are now seen as fitting into the nationalities associated with those kings at that particular point of Bible history. One example is the Amorite king Arioch, referred to in Genesis 14:1. From Mari we read of a king with this name, rendered as Arriwuk. About twenty thousand tablets were recovered from Mari and they threw considerable light on military, diplomatic, and administrative affairs about the time of Abraham.

The tablets reveal that the people of Mari traded far and wide, for this city was at the crossroads of trade routes that stretched out to the north, south, east, and west. It becomes clear that journeys such as Abraham's, as recorded in the Bible, were relatively common in patriarchal times.

In his journeys, Abraham would have followed regular trade routes, and a confirmation of that is the association in the patriarchal records of Ur with the city of Haran. Ur and Haran were both centers of moon worship. They had cultural connections, and it is probable that Abraham's forefathers were moon-worshipers. In Joshua 24:2 it is made clear that Abraham's forebears had worshiped other gods — "on the other side of the river" (the river was the Euphrates, not "the flood," as the King James Version mistakenly renders it).

Almost all the cities associated with Abraham in the Bible records are now known, either from archaeological excavations or from nonbiblical writings. Ancient centers thrived at different times, and if a particular center was occupied, it would be likely for a nearby city to be deserted. The accuracy of the biblical narrative in the selection of the correct towns is a clear pointer to the eyewitness nature of the original records.

Another indication of geographic accuracy is that when Abraham moved around Palestine, the northern areas had been deserted to a great extent because of the hostile activity of the Amorites, invaders from the west. A series of about 7,200 potsherds, known as the Sethe Texts (after the translater, Kurt Sethe), refer to about twenty Palestine-Syria districts and to about thirty of the chiefs associated with those areas.[38] These, together with the Berlin Execration Texts (cursing texts) dating to 1926 B.C., show that only a few towns were occupied in central Palestine. Such texts were written on figurines or clay vessels, and when the vessels were smashed, the written curse was supposedly released against the persons named thereon. About a century later, as the Brussels Texts show, there were many more towns, and again the personal names used were Amorite. The society of the area was changing from seminomadic to the more settled form of life that, as we now know from the Ebla tablets, earlier settlers had previously enjoyed. Abraham entered Palestine just at the time when this change was taking place. That explains why Abraham moved about so much, but by the time of his grandson Jacob, life was much more settled.

We have already referred to the archaeological evidence endorsing the general picture given in Genesis 14, where there is a record of the battle of four kings against five. Surface surveys carried out by W. F. Albright and Nelson Glueck show that a Bronze Age trade route ran through the Transjordan area referred to in Genesis 14.[39] A line of Middle Bronze Age fortresses skirts this trade route, and the Bible incident fits clearly into that background. An interesting pointer to the eyewitness nature of the biblical records is that in the biblical account some of the places are given their modern names as well as the ancient ones, e.g., "Bela which is Zoar." There was such respect for these documents that they would not be altered under any circumstances. An editing note was added to make things clear to a later generation, but the records themselves were not altered.

The same chapter tells of Abraham recovering his nephew Lot, and we read of Abraham having 318 *hanikim*. The term is used only here in the Bible, and it was unknown at the time when the King James Version was translated in the early seventeenth century. It was rightly guessed to mean "trained servants," and the word is now known in other records such as Egyptian Execration Texts. It literally means "retainers" (trained servants). Thus it would seem that Abraham had a private army. Other people had such private armies, this being shown by an inspection that took place in the City of Ur at the time of the Third Dynasty, about 2000 B.C. One tablet lists the private armies that were reviewed by the commissioner of the city, and

these groups are given in detail. They vary in size from
40 to 600 people, the average being about 300. An
important trader such as Abraham, with very large
flocks and herds, would undoubtedly have a large
number of retainers, as the record in Genesis indicates.

**Further Histor-
ical Evidence**

There are many other evidences pointing to the
historicity of the patriarchal narratives. Books on biblical archaeology constantly refer to the famous Nuzi

*One of the Nuzi tab-
lets that helped to
establish the historic-
ity of some of the
patriarchal narra-
tives.*

tablets, recovered by the team led by Dr. Chiera of the
American Schools of Oriental Research, beginning in
1925.[40] About twenty thousand tablets were recovered, though many had been bored through by
worms (the original bookworms!). Although these tablets do not date back to patriarchal times, they do give
many examples of customs that had prevailed over
long periods of time and they throw considerable light
on the records in the second half of Genesis. As a result
of the findings based on these and other recovered
tablets, scholars have long ago abandoned the idea
mentioned earlier that the patriarchal records are
reflections from the period of the divided kingdom
after Solomon. All scholarship now at least acknowl-

edges what is often called "the substantial historicity"
of the patriarchal narratives, and many go farther to
declare their complete accuracy. As long ago as 1940,
Albright wrote concerning "so many corroborations of
details" that most competent scholars gave up the
earlier critical view that the patriarchal stories actually
reflected the ninth through eighth centuries B.C.[41] The
tide has continued to flow towards increasing acceptance of biblical accuracy.

Laws of inheritance, rights of adoption, the rights of
secondary wives, and even the use of jewelry, such as
golden earrings, all point to the factual nature of the
Bible records about Abraham and his descendents.
Even the record of the purchase of a tomb for Sarah,
recorded in Genesis 23, once seen as a legendary story
to explain the tradition about Abraham and Sarah being
buried in the cave of Machpelah, is now accepted as
accurate history. This story is similar at a number of
points to other records recovered from the ancient
Hittites and appears to be a narrative description of an
actual Hittite contract. The biblical record displays an
intimate knowledge of Hittite laws and customs and
fits very well into the patriarchal period. It was probably a narrative summary of an actual legal document
drawn up between Abraham and the Hittite from whom
he bought the property.[42] The very existence of the
Hittite people was challenged a generation ago, but
now all that is changed. The excavations at the Hittite
capital of Boghazkoy (ancient Hattusas, now modern
Turkey) have demonstrated the great importance of the
early Hittite people. Their history dates approximately
to Abraham's time (about 2000 B.C.).[43]

Even the sensational story of the destruction of
Sodom and Gomorrah is no longer seen as arising from
the realm of romantic tales. Surface surveys undertaken in the old Transjordan area, on the east side of the
Dead Sea, have revealed a series of five ancient cities
dating back to Middle Bronze times, each situated
alongside a wadi (stream), with various evidences of
civilization, including some burial sites. The reconstruction of this incident points to earthquake activity,
and the evidence is strong that the various layers of the
earth were disrupted and hurled high into the air.

Bitumen is plentiful there, and a good pictorial description would be to say that brimstone (bituminous pitch) was hurled down on those cities that had rejected God. There is evidence that the layers of sedimentary rock have been molded together by intense heat. Evidence of such burning has been found on the top of the nearby Jebel Usdum (Mount Sodom). This is a permanent evidence of the great conflagration that took place in the long-distant past, possibly when an oil basin beneath the Dead Sea ignited and erupted. In addition to this topographical data, the recent discovery at Ebla gives additional extrabiblical confirmation to the existence of the five cities of the plain.[44] Every one of the cities is mentioned in the Ebla tablets, and each was a trading center. This immediately puts an end to speculation that this was nothing but a romantic tale. Even the geographical order of the cities is reflected in the biblical listing.

Although natural cause seems to be indicated by the heat-fused rock and bituminous pitch, such natural means are in no way incompatible with the biblical explanation of God's judgment. The providential element is the timing of the event, which followed the refusal of all appeals to repentance. Sometimes figurative language is used in the description of events in the Bible. This was so in the description of "fire and brimstone" being rained down. The fiery pitch probably first came from the reservoirs of bitumen near the earth's surface, so that it was hurled into the air and then came down as "fire and brimstone" rained from heaven. What goes up must come down, and this picturesque description is entirely satisfactory. We use such figurative language today, even in simple expressions such as "the sun rose." The sun, of course, does not rise, for it is the earth that rotates in relation to the sun.

Even incidents such as Rachel's stealing her father's clay gods (his *teraphim*) have now become recognized as authentic historical incidents, for the Nuzi documents show that such clay gods were virtually title deeds to property.[45] Before she stole the clay gods, Rachel joined her sister Leah in saying, "Is there any inheritance left for us in our father's house?" (Gen.

*Teraphim (clay fig-
urines of gods) were
used as title deeds
to property. These,
found at Nuzi, may
be similar to the ones
Rachel stole from her
father.*

31:14). Her father had treated them shabbily, so she
took the law into her own hands, entered his tent in his
absence, and took the teraphim—the title deeds.

Esau's sale of his birthright for a bowl of food has
always marked him out as the least likely to succeed,
the story perplexing most readers. However, it too
makes sense in the light of the same Nuzi tablets, for in
them we read of one man who sold his portion of the
inheritance for three sheep.

The fact is that the patriarchal narratives are not
reflections of a later age, nor are they the end result of
stories told around campfires and embellished with the
telling. They are factual records set in a period of
history that has become increasingly understood in the
light of the archaeological discoveries of this century.[46] History has welcomed their contribution at last.

Chapter Notes

chapter four

The Land of
the Pharaohs

Many evidences of Egyptian culture in the biblical story of Israel in Egypt authenticate the biblical account of this crucible experience.

It should not surprise us that the Egyptians say little about the Hebrews. It is widely believed that when Joseph was made the chief ruler in the land, foreigners were in control. When these foreigners (the Hyksos rulers) were thrown out of Egypt, every attempt was made to purge references to this period. The Egyptian people themselves regarded this time as "the great abomination."

Most historians agree there was a second "Intermediate Period"—between the Egyptian Middle Kingdom and the New Kingdom, and that this second Intermediate Period covered the time that the Hyksos rulers were in power. It seems likely that this is the time when Joseph and his family came into Egypt. There are some interesting factors pointing to their association with the Hyksos. The Hyksos people were Semites, of the same ethnic stock as the Hebrews.[47] It seems that the Hyksos rulers retained much of the internal administrative procedures of the Egyptians themselves and kept many local Egyptian officials in the positions that they had previously occupied. That might explain why in the first five verses of Genesis 39 Potiphar is three times called an "Egyptian." If the local Egyptians were still ruling, it would hardly make sense to refer to an official as "the Egyptian."

Joseph in Egypt

The records about Joseph are not known in Egyptian sources; doubtless they would have been included in those that were eliminated when the Hyksos were overthrown. However, many interesting pieces of local color and Egyptian words are embedded in the Joseph narratives, so much so that it is widely recognized that these stories are not folklore, but actual records set against the background of Egypt in the times referred to in the Bible.[48] In them it is said that Joseph was made the overseer of his master's house, and the word *merper* ("overseer") is correctly used.

There are various other titles also correctly used, such as "chief butler" and "chief baker," both in chapter 40. Then in 41:40–43, there is a report of how Joseph was installed as the vizier, or first officer of the land. The installation procedures described in Genesis are remarkably similar to those known from recovered Egyptian documents. The royal signet ring of authority, the gold chain of office, and the fine linen clothes, all attest to the eyewitness nature of the records.[49]

Even Joseph's new name of Zaphnath-Paaneah, meaning "Head of the Sacred College" (sometimes translated as "Revealer of Secrets"), is known in Egypt, though at a later time. It is highly probable that the Bible has the first recorded use of this particular title.

Joseph was made the civil head of the Egyptian government and the religious leader of Egypt as well. It was a remarkable position, but not entirely without precedent, for there are records of other people of lowly birth, such as Canaanite slaves, being promoted to high positions in Egypt.[50]

The very first mention of the horse in the Bible is in Genesis 47:17, when the Egyptians sold their horses to buy corn. This fits the background, for it was the Hyksos rulers who utilized horses so widely in their conquest and rule of Egypt.

We also read that Joseph was given the Pharaoh's second chariot and that the people "bowed the knee" before him. This is in keeping with the Hyksos' use of chariots, for they had introduced the light chariot of war into Egypt. This was one of the major means by which they conquered the Egyptians and other peoples.

Joseph's brothers eventually came to Egypt to buy corn, and after certain preliminary tests, Joseph introduced himself to them. In Genesis 45:8 we read that he used three titles: "Father (or Adviser) to Pharaoh," "Lord of Pharaoh's House," and "Ruler of all Egypt."[51] The first title is actually "Father to the Gods," for the Pharaoh was supposedly the manifestation of Ra, the sun god, but Joseph could not use that title in its Egyptian form, so he Hebraized it and made it "Father to Pharaoh." Joseph was the Pharaoh's personal adviser, in charge of palace affairs, and he was the ruler of both upper and lower Egypt. The titles he mentioned were actual titles known to us now from ancient Egypt.

It is interesting that at that time the Pharaoh was not necessarily known by his name, but simply by his title, the Pharaoh (literally, "the Great House").[52] In later history, especially in the times of the New Kingdom, the Pharaoh was more often known by his actual name. This also is in keeping with the Bible records where we read of such Pharaohs as Necho, Tirhakah, and Sheshonk (Shishak).

The Impress of Egyptian Culture

Many other Egyptian references in the story of Joseph make it clear that the record was set in Egypt and was not put in writing hundreds of years later, as critics claimed earlier this century. Even recorded practices of magic and embalming have an Egyptian flavor, and there are various points at which such references are quietly introduced into the text. In themselves they are virtually unimportant, but added together, they make a valuable contribution and assure us that these records were first put in writing when Joseph was in Egypt. This is not surprising, for in his time even slaves were occasionally known to write their names and other personal details on the walls of buildings. It is clearly reasonable to expect that an administrator such as Joseph would keep good records.

This Bible drama was no fairy tale played out in a land of shadows. These were actual men of flesh and blood who lived and planned, who bought and sold, and made their journeys. There is a constant reminder that the records are those of eyewitnesses.

Ultimately, the native Egyptians overthrew the Hyksos and drove them out. This is probably the background to the statement "Now there arose a new king who knew not Joseph" (Exod. 1:8). In those first eight verses of Exodus, hundreds of years of history are recorded. The history of the Bible is not always detailed but is a selection according to the divine purposes in the presentation of truth.

When the Hyksos were deposed from ruling positions, the non-Egyptians became slaves. Eventually Moses was born, and the story of his adoption by the Pharaoh's daughter is well known.

A papyrus from Egypt with a list of slaves, including Hebrews, about the time of Joseph. Approximately forty-five Semitic names like Jacob, Issachar, Asher, Job, and Joseph are given.

chapter five

From Slavery to Nationhood

Moses and the Law are assessed in light of contentions that the Law was of much later origin than the biblical claim. Comparison to covenant forms in use in the mid–second millennium B.C. indicate the authenticity of the Bible's claim.

It was Moses who eventually led the children of Israel out of captivity to freedom. As the late G. Ernest Wright stated, "The exodus from Egyptian slavery was a dominant and dominating event in Israel history and faith."[53] The date of the Exodus remains a contested issue. This survey is not the place to enter into a discussion of the date, for the evidence is not conclusive, either in the Bible or from archaeological excavations. At first sight it seems that the Bible does give a specific date, for 1 Kings 6:1 says that the Exodus took place 480 years before the fourth year of Solomon's reign. However, there are three variants of that verse, and the figures vary by forty years each. It is therefore sometimes argued that the figure is really a totaling of generations, not the actual number of years—that twelve generations are added together, covering the 49 same period referred to in 1 Chronicles 6:1–10.[54]

J. A. Thompson and Merrill Unger (as shown in references 2 and 3 of chapter 1) have each summarized the evidence in their separate books on archaeology and the Old Testament. Unger leans more toward an early date than does Thompson, but each recognizes the problem. It is entirely likely that this is an area where the archaeological conclusions will be modified: some problems of pottery dating (as observed by this author at the excavation of Gezer in 1969) might point to the need for reassessment of dating of some civilizations going back to the end of the Late Bronze Age and the Early Iron Age. This is the approximate time of the Exodus from Egypt and the conquest of Canaan. Archaeological dating is not "absolute" in relation to many such areas, and it is not irrelevant to state that biblical evidence has stood firm while archaeological interpretations have undergone change (e.g., as to the date of the early level of Jericho excavated by Sir John Garstang).[55]

Moses and the Law

The historicity of the early nationhood of Israel is shown in the giving of the law. This took place when the Hebrews came to Mount Sinai, where they received their law through Moses. Various law codes have been rediscovered, and it is no longer seriously argued that Moses could not have recorded a code of laws so early. Law codes are known from as early as 2000 B.C., associated with Ur-Nammu of the Third Dynasty of Ur; and there were others, such as that of Bilalama of Eshnunna, of Lipit-Ishtar, and of Hammurabi of Babylon.[56]

Occasionally the teachings in the law of Moses have noticeable similarities to some of those codes, an example being that punishment was to be meted out in the case of personal injuries caused by one man to another. The similarities probably arose from common social conditions. Although Moses would have been aware of earlier law codes, this does not in any way

A stele of Ham-murabi from Susa with a law code in-scribed.

interfere with the fact of inspiration, but rather implies that the documents were genuinely set against the background claimed for them.[57]

While the similarities indicate that the laws of Moses came from that time period, the dissimilarities point to the superiority of Moses' laws, especially regarding moral and spiritual concepts. One example is that incest is dealt with much more leniently in the code of Hammurabi than by Moses, and Hammurabi had punishments that varied according to social status. Hammurabi decreed that if a nobleman knocked out the tooth of another nobleman of the same rank, they should knock out his tooth; but, if it was the tooth of a commoner, he would merely pay one-third of a mina of silver. (The tooth fairy could do better!) With the law code of Moses it was an eye for an eye, and a tooth for a tooth. Moses introduced the concept of equality, something that was unknown in codes such as that of Hammurabi.

For more than a century, a critical view of the writings of Moses—the first five books of the Bible, also called the Pentateuch—has enjoyed popularity. Known as the "documentary hypothesis," this view set forth the contention that two or more original sources were woven by a redactor, or editor (probably a priest), to form our present Pentateuch. Elaborations of the theory multiply the number of original authors. The net effect of the theory, of course, is that the authenticity and integrity of these documents are undermined.

One important evidence of the genuineness of the Mosaic writings has come from the researches of George Mendenhall of the University of Michigan. His writings have been reported in various places, one good summary being in *The Bible and the Ancient Near East.*[58] Mendenhall makes the point that a seemingly endless stream of details indicates that these narratives belong to the Bronze Age. (Abraham is dated to the "Middle Bronze Age" and Moses to "Late Bronze.") He points out that the consequences to the historian are enormous. Israel's beginnings as a nation were set in a period that is now known, and her neighbors are also to a great extent understood. Mendenhall suggests that there were many seemingly incidental or accidental details recorded in the patriarchal records and that the narratives contained names and specific forms of cultic actions, patterns of thought, and "concrete cultural features which can be checked by extra-biblical sources."

Mendenhall has made an outstanding contribution to the study of Mosaic authorship. He recognizes that because of the evidences that have come forward in the last forty years, scholars have become increasingly aware that the records of Genesis cannot be dismissed as Canaanite myths. He also argues that Moses took the Book of the Covenant (Exod. 20–31) and read it in the audience of the people.[59] This reference to an actual book for reading to the people is the straightforward statement of the Bible itself, at such places as Exodus 17:14; 24:4,7, Deuteronomy 31:9, and (later) Ezra 8:1ff.

The Unity of Moses' Writings

Various covenant documents relating to the neighbors of the Hebrew people have been recovered, and Mendenhall has undertaken a great deal of research on those documents. He compares the Mosaic writings with those of other people, especially the Hittites. The Hebrew covenants as recorded by Moses make sense only when they are seen as a unity, a unity dating back to the times of Moses. Mendenhall's hypothesis has again demonstrated that the Book of the Covenant does not endorse the documentary hypothesis with its patchwork of strands, supposedly brought together over hundreds of years.

The Book of the Covenant bears the pattern of Hittite "suzerainty covenants."[60] Such Hittite suzerainty covenants had a remarkably consistent pattern and included six major points, as follows:

1. The author of the covenant is identified in the *preamble*.
2. In the *historical prologue* previous dealings or relationships between the parties are outlined, including the reasons why the vassal should be

grateful for past blessings, and so be prepared to undertake obedience in the future.

3. Basic *stipulations* are laid down by the sovereign, to be accepted by the vassal.

4. A copy of the covenant is to be *deposited* in the sanctuary of the vassal, and the people are to be acquainted with the terms of the covenant by a *periodic public reading*.

5. A number of gods are invoked as *witnesses* to the covenant.

6. If the vassal breaks the covenant, *curses* are invoked on him, whereas if he keeps the covenant he will experience *blessings*.

This is essentially the pattern that is followed with the covenant entered into with the children of Israel, although there are variations because of the distinctive nature of the Hebrew people and their relationship to their God. While the concept of "witnesses" is clearly there, the children of Israel could not invoke pagan gods as witnesses, so memorial stones were used instead, or the people themselves would be the witnesses.

In *Ancient Orient and the Old Testament,* Kenneth Kitchen analyzes the Sinai covenant to show how it fits the above pattern. He then states, "It is strikingly evident that the Sinai covenant and its renewals *must* be classed with the late-second-millennium covenants."[61] The covenant itself is recorded in Exodus 20–31; after an idolatrous interlude, by which the covenant was broken, it was renewed, as shown in Exodus 34. It was once again renewed with the new generation after the wilderness journey, as shown in Deuteronomy 1–32:47. Finally, Joshua again presents it in chapter 24 of the book bearing his name.

Kitchen discusses the implications of all this to the writing of the covenant documents in Exodus, Leviticus, Deuteronomy, and Joshua. Having analyzed the covenant forms in the second and first millennia, he shows that "there are clear and undeniable differences," both as to the form and the content. He then shows that the documentary hypothesis—which denies the authenticity of the Mosaic covenant on dating grounds — simply does not make sense in the light of this material. If the documents were not committed to writing (as claimed by the documentary hypothesis) until the ninth to sixth centuries B.C. and beyond, it is strange that writers or redactors would so easily reproduce the biblical covenant form that had fallen out of customary usage some three to six hundred years earlier.

That is not all. Not only do the biblical documents fit the literary mold of the period that the Bible itself claims for them, but they also defy the covenant forms in common use at the time the documentary hypothesis claims for their writing.

It is fair to ask if the documentary hypothesis would have retained any credibility if it had been related to any book other than the Bible. That Book has withstood hammering blows through the centuries, and the unsubstantiated blows of this hypothesis have possibly rung the loudest: perhaps because of the hollowness of its arguments.

**More About
Covenant Forms**

Others besides Kitchen have taken up Mendenhall's thesis, and today it has gained wide acceptance among archaeologists and Old Testament scholars.

In *New Directions in Biblical Archaeology* G. Ernest Wright wrote a stimulating article entitled "Biblical Archaeology Today." Among his interesting conclusions is one relating to the patriarchs; he states that the patriarchal period is at last beginning to emerge into a setting that is known in Near Eastern history.[62]

He then discusses Mendenhall's pioneer work on the formal background of the Mosaic covenant. A similar style is to be found specifically in the suzerainty treaties, found among the archives of the Hittites and dating to the Late Bronze Age. Wright also points out that another major conclusion from this new knowledge is that God is not presented in the Bible as the head of a pantheon, identified with the primary powers of the natural world. Rather, He was the Suzerain— the King of Kings and the Lord of Lords, having no equal.

In that same volume Albright also stressed the significance of Mendenhall's discovery that there is a close analogy between the structure of the early covenant between Jehovah and Israel and the Hittite suzerainty treaties at the time of Moses.[63]

Some of these matters were outlined in a lecture by Wright to the personnel excavating at Gezer in 1969, referred to earlier. Afterwards a small group of us discussed the implications of this new discovery with Wright. He emphasized that Mendenhall's conclusions should be accepted, and that his work had radically altered the attitude of many scholars towards the date and writing of the Mosaic "Book of the Covenant."

All this highlights the way in which Moses has come back into "respectability" with a wide spectrum of scholars who have been involved in archaeological research. In 1959 J. Vergote of Paris published his *Joseph en Egypt*. He was certainly not setting out to "prove" the Bible, but after analyzing so many of the Egyptianisms and local color in the settings of the Joseph and Moses stories, he came to the conclusion that not only must the record be dated back to the time of Moses but that it is also a unity. This is the same conclusion, although from a different approach, that Mendenhall and others have reached on a parallel matter relating to Moses.

Perhaps it is also relevant to state in passing that the supposed borrowing by Moses of monotheism from Amenhotep IV (the infamous Ikhnaten) has now been discounted. Ikhnaten ruthlessly destroyed those who opposed his concept of "monotheism," but as soon as he died, polytheism was reintroduced into Egypt. Ikhnaten himself was branded as "the great heretic," and his religious views were put aside. In any case, Ikhnaten did not really put forward monotheism, for his view was that Ra, the sun god, was the one true god, and that as he was the manifestation of Ra, the people should worship Ra and himself. His was the worship of two gods—the impersonal sun and himself. This was dramatically different from the concept that Moses put forward. Moses did not suggest the worship of an impersonal power such as the sun, and, as we read the accounts of Moses, we recognize that he most certainly did not ask for personal worship.

The so-called monotheism of Ikhnaten was also greatly different in its basic concepts from that of Moses, for Moses taught his people that Yahweh was the one true God, the holy God who demanded that His people be holy. This association of God with holiness and morality was a Hebrew concept. The Hebrews gave to the world this one almighty God who challenged His people to partake of His holy character. This unique presentation was the true monotheism that only Moses and the Hebrew people knew in the ancient world.

Chapter Notes

"Joshua Fit the Battle of Jericho" – and Other Battles Too!

The problem of dating the Exodus is touched on. The conquest of Canaan is clearly seen. Excavations at Jericho, Hazor, Lachish, Eglon, Debir, and other cities of Canaan show a common sequence: Canaanite culture, fire, and a cruder Israelite culture built over the rubble.

When Moses died, his right-hand man, Joshua, was challenged to take over the leadership: "Moses my servant is dead: you therefore arise and go over this Jordan, you and all the people of Israel, into the land I will give you" (Josh. 1:2).

The Israelites had to cross the River Jordan without boats, for these were a desert people who had spent their lifetimes in a wilderness journey. We read that the waters of the Jordan were blocked from Adam (the modern Damieh), about sixteen miles north of Jericho (Josh. 3). Three times in relatively modern history   59

(1266, 1906, and 1927) a landslide has been reported at this narrow point of the Jordan, and has blocked its flow. John Garstang, one of the early excavators of Jericho, recorded having seen the effect of the landslide of 1927, and this was reported in international newspapers. On that particular occasion the Jordan stopped flowing for over twenty-one hours, and thousands of people could have crossed the river on foot.

Sometimes the miracles of the Bible are miracles of synchronization, or timing. If God is in control of the forces of nature, He can cause those forces to be brought together at the right moment of time to fulfill His purposes.

We do not suggest that that is the complete answer. In a survey dealing with the reliability of the Bible, it would be quite wrong to suggest that all the incidents of the Bible can be explained by natural phenomena or natural causes. The Bible is not only a book of history, it is also a book showing God's dealings with mankind. It should not be necessary to invoke natural causes for all the miracles. With a proper approach to the Bible, one should be open to its concept that there is a God who is almighty, and who can use or ignore the forces of nature as He works. Belief in the concept of an all-powerful God involves belief in the miraculous; God would be able to cause His own forces to come together at the right moment of time, or, if it suits His intents, to go beyond those laws to accomplish His purposes.

Another example is found in the record of the destruction of Jericho. Its walls have fallen down some seventeen times, apparently by earthquake activity. Once again, synchronization might well have been involved in this miraculous activity. If the miraculous is to be ruled out, the army of Israel must have indeed been surprised when the walls came down! What serendipity! No, rather these men expected the walls to fall down, as a point of faith, when they marched around that beseiged city (at a sensible distance, because of the archers on the walls!). When they had done their part, as commanded by God, at the right moment the walls collapsed. God was in control of His own forces, and His purposes came to pass at the critical moment.

When Jericho was excavated by the British archaeologist Sir John Garstang in the 1930s, he reported that he had found a city level corresponding to the conquest of Joshua. But later excavations by Kathleen Kenyon suggested that Garstang had wrongly identified this level and that there was a small area associated with a later level that should be dated to the time of Joshua. Great controversy raged for some years, but these days a modifying position has been accepted. It seems there was a merging of levels—as can happen in the development of a site—and that Garstang had clearly confused two levels. He also ignored some pointers to a later civilization, such as a cemetery outside the city that did not coincide with the level he personally identified as that of Joshua's time.

Neolithic street level in excavated Jericho.

There are some aspects of the conquest of Canaan that present problems for the relationship between the Bible records and archaeological findings. The position is quite interesting and perhaps unique. It should be recognized that the Bible records are not always detailed statements of history in the modern Western sense. Our modern way is to give all the details in a systematic and chronological presentation. That was not always so in the Bible records, for the Hebrews were showing history as God-controlled activity. Therefore only selections of history are given; as Merrill F. Unger says, "The events recorded in the biblical account are evidently highly selective."[64] The datings are not always given in terms of years, as in modern history reporting, but where they are so given it has been amazing to see how modern research has endorsed those figures—illustrated especially in Edwin R. Thiele's book *The Mysterious Numbers of the Hebrew Kings.*[65] When we come to the story of the conquest, some things are not quite as precisely recorded as they are in that period of the divided kingdom that Thiele is especially treating in his book.

We have earlier referred to the problem of the date of the Exodus from Egypt, and that is also relevant in a consideration of the conquest of Canaan. If the Exodus was about 1440 B.C., then the conquest of Canaan began somewhere about 1400; if the Exodus is to be dated at 1290/70, then the conquest must be dated at 1250/30. Good scholarship is lined up on both sides, and we will not defer from our major topic to seek to resolve the problem. However, it might be well to point out here that when seeming discrepancies occur between the Bible and archaeology, a judicious response would be to withhold judgment. Historically, many have leaped to pronounce sentence while the jury was still out, only to find that later archaeological discoveries resolved the conflict.

The pattern of conquest in the Book of Joshua indicates that the land of Canaan was not controlled by any single king at that time, but there were various city states, each with a king controlling a limited amount of territory. Jericho, Hazor, Lachish, and a number of other cities are each shown to have had separate kings, no doubt controlling the immediate area as well. The famous Amarna Letters show that this pattern of city states was later modified and that kings came to control considerably larger areas.[66]

While recognizing the dating problems referred to above, it is relevant to point out that various aspects of the conquest have been endorsed. Archaeologists recognize that the last word has not yet been said about the dating of the Early Iron Age in Israel (Joshua's time). This is one point at which the Bible itself is used by archaeologists as a point of cross-reference and as a sourcebook. Nelson Glueck often said (as at the Gezer excavation in 1969) that he excavated with a trowel in one hand and a Bible in the other. Just as Garstang used the Bible's clues for the identification of Hazor,[67] so the Bible clues will eventually help solve other problems relative to the Exodus, where, at present, only a general pattern of agreement can be shown.

One example relates to three of the fortress cities defeated by Joshua in the area of the Shephelah, the southern entrance to the land proper. The fortress cities of Lachish, Eglon, and Debir have been excavated, and the archaeological evidence shows that they have a typical pattern of destruction, presumably by Joshua, within that general time period. They had the same crude building pattern that has been found at other cities associated with Joshua's conquest—there was a level of burning over a Canaanite city, with the cruder Israelite culture on top of that burning.[68] Wright describes another good example of this pattern at Bethel in his book *Biblical Archaeology*.

As we said, there are various indicators pointing to the general pattern described in the Bible. Thus, in Joshua 11:10 the city of Hazor is described as "head of all those kingdoms," and the excavations by Yigael Yadin show that the site occupied some two hundred acres and that the population would have been about forty thousand.[69] Hazor was destroyed violently and was reoccupied at about the same time as the cities referred to above, and in general terms this fits the biblical description. The Bible does not set out to give an exhaustive, detailed statement, as shown by a study of Joshua 12; a list of kings and of cities conquered in the center of the land is given, but elaborate details are not. The conquest was clearly not completed in Joshua's lifetime, though the land itself was conquered. Some of the unconquered towns are referred to in Joshua 17:11–13 and Judges 1:26–27. They include Bethshan and Megiddo, and excavation at both these sites indicates that they remained in Canaanite hands at the time that the cities referred to above were conquered. Such negative evidence is as relevant as the positive evidence of destruction.

The ruins of Hazor, a city that Joshua burned.

Some aspects relating to the destruction of the Canaanites are outside historical perspectives, in that spiritual values enter. However, it is pertinent that archaeological excavation makes it clear that at the time of the conquest the Canaanites practiced all sorts of abominations opposed to the spiritual principles associated with the incoming Israelites.[70] The formal worship of the Canaanites included debased sexual practices, and children were even sacrificed in funerary jars, buried at the foundations of temples and other buildings.

Against that context, God ordered the destruction of those people who would be a spiritual cancer in the midst of His people. The time of judgment had come, and, no matter how reliable we see the history of the Bible, this does not alter the fact that spiritual concepts are also associated with this book. Old and New Testaments alike present God as a God of judgment, and when His mercy is rejected, judgment must fall. Throughout the Scriptures that is shown consistently as a principle of God's dealings with men. The great Flood, the ten judgments on the people of Egypt, and now the judgment on the Canaanites all illustrate the same principle.

The Bible writers are informed as to the gods of the nations surrounding them. Thus we read in Judges 2:11–14 that in the generation following Joshua many Israelites forsook the Lord and served Baal and Asherah, Canaanite deities. This accurate knowledge of the gods of neighboring peoples is seen often in both Old and New Testaments—e.g., the Philistine corn god Dagon (1 Sam. 5:2), Bel and Nebo of the Babylonians (Isa. 46:1), and Diana (Artemis in Greek) of the Ephesians (Acts 19:28). This is another area where the local color is demonstrably authentic and points to eyewitness reporting.

Chapter Notes

chapter seven

The Kingdom Is Established

Field work has shed light on the unifying confederation of Israel's tribes. The excavation of Philistine houses, Saul's fortress at Gibeah, the temple at Bethshan, and others have contributed to our understanding of the confederation. The rise of David and Israel's territorial, military, and economic stabilization are witnessed in the archaeological record.

After recording the death of Joshua, the Bible introduces us to the period of the Judges. It is often said that at this time Israel was an amphictyonic league—a loose confederation of tribes united for a purpose. Their unity depended on their covenant with Jehovah, the law of Moses, their one language, and their central sanctuary situated at Shiloh. (There were also local centers of worship.)

It is of historical significance to notice that at this time the Israelite houses were poorly constructed, having small stones to fill holes in the walls and rooms added as the occupants were able to find the materials to make extensions possible. There was little evidence of planning. Their pottery was poorly fired, whereas 67 that of the Canaanites was of a high standard. Even the fortifications built by the Israelites were crude and thin compared to the massive structures of the Canaanites whose centers they had taken.[71] That was the general pattern until the time of David, when rapid changes were introduced and efficient fortifications became commonplace.

Various other interesting historical points may be mentioned in passing, such as the fact that the Israelites had to contact the Philistines, for the Philistines had a monopoly on the smelting of iron until the time of Saul. In 1 Samuel 13:19–21, we find that the Philistines would not allow a blacksmith to operate in Israelite territory, "lest the Hebrews fashion swords or spears for themselves." Smelting furnaces have been found on the borders of Philistine territory at Tell Qasile, Tell Jemmeh, and Beth Shemesh.[72]

Another interesting cultural point relates to the Philistine drinking habits, for many of their jugs have been found, complete with strainer spouts to hold back the barley husks. This fits the background of the story of Samson, in which the drinking practices of the Philistines are implied in their "high spirits" at the festival for their god Dagon (Judg. 16:23–25). Albright makes the point that the Philistines were "mighty carousers."[73] Similarly, Samson's pulling down the central pillars of a house are not as incredible as a previous generation would have thought. At Tell Qasile, at Tel'Afula, and at Sarahun, various Philistine houses have been excavated, with courtyards surrounding the central roofed building, which had rows of pillars to support the roof. Exceptionally strong men such as Samson could have destroyed structures like these by collapsing the central pillars.[74]

The Philistines were among the most powerful of the enemies that the Israelites encountered, and their attacks became more persistent in the days of Samuel. Even in his childhood they captured the ark of the covenant, and archaeological evidence suggests that they destroyed the sanctuary at Shiloh at this time.[75] This destruction probably fits the happenings referred to in 1 Samuel 4 and Jeremiah 7:12–14; 26:6–9.

When Samuel was old and the people saw that his sons did not follow his example, they began to ask for "a king like all the nations" (1 Sam. 8:5). Archaeology throws a great deal of light on the impending oppression of the Israelites, for to have "a king like all the nations" would mean military conscription, the confiscation of their personal lands, the introduction of heavy taxation, and forced labor. That is the picture we get from Canaanite documents found at Alalakh and Ras Shamra.

Despite the warnings of the now-aged Samuel, the people were determined. Conceding to their wishes, the Lord chose Saul to be their first king. Saul had great physical attractions, but was not "a man after God's own heart." He started well, but soon gave evidence of becoming faithless; and so Israel had, indeed, "a king like all the nations." He took to himself forbidden priestly offices and was guilty of grave failure in spiritual principles. He began to put himself above the LORD, and this was far from the ordained pattern of kingship in Israel.

Israel was never meant to be other than a theocracy. God Himself was to be their King, and though there was a human king, he was to be the vicegerent of God. The king was supposedly God's representative, and the Scriptures tell us that eventually God rejected Saul because of his folly.

One interesting archaeological point from the time of Saul relates to the fortress he constructed at Gibeah, a few miles north of Jerusalem. Beginning in 1922, it was excavated by Albright. It proved to be a citadel with two stories and a massive stairway that led to the upstairs section where Saul himself had probably lived.[76] There were double protective walls; the outer wall was about five feet thick, while the inner wall was some four feet thick. The excavators found earthenware vessels that had been used for the storage of commodities like grain, wine, and oil.

There were other objects, such as rubbing stones for grinding flour, the iron point of an ancient plough, and typical weapons from Saul's times, including bronze arrowheads and stone slingshots. These last were very important, as shown by heaps of such stones at various places and battle scenes cut into stone depicting their use. Slingshots were carefully prepared and polished by ancient warriors—illustrated, for example, by those recovered at Tell Beit Mirsim.[77] There were also written records from surrounding peoples that referred to such slingshots. That is the background of Judges 20:16, where we read of seven hundred left-handed slingers who were so accurate that they could sling their stones with hairbreadth precision.

Saul's fortress at Gibeah, referred to above, was strongly built, but it was crude by the standard of later Israelite buildings. That is not surprising, for Israel was still in its early tribal stage. Archaeology shows that there were great improvements in building constructions at later times, especially in the times of David and Solomon.

The Death of King Saul

Another important contact between the Israelites and the Philistines took place at the battle on Mount Gilboa when Saul and his sons were killed. In 1 Samuel 31:10 we learn that after Saul's death, his armor was put in the temple of the goddess Ashtaroth at nearby Bethshan, whereas in 1 Chronicles 10:10 we are told that his head was put in the temple of Dagon, the Philistine corn god. The temple of Bethshan was excavated in the 1920s, prior to which some scholars thought that the reference to these two temples was in error, for Ashtaroth was a Canaanite goddess whereas Dagon was a Philistine grain god: would enemy peoples each have a temple at the same level of occupation (Level V, dating to about the eleventh century B.C.)? The excavations uncovered two temples separated by a corridor. In one of them an Ashtaroth figurine was found. The conquering Philistines had apparently absorbed the Canaanite goddess into their own pantheon, and this record about the death of Saul therefore has remarkable evidence of local color.[78]

By now Israel was ready for a united kingdom. The possibility of attack was a constant threat. Even before the reign of King Saul, it became evident that unity was necessary if the nation's independence was to be main-

Bethshan tell. The
findings here explain
how Saul's armor
could have been put
in a temple of both
the goddess Ashta-
roth and the god
Dagon.

tained in times of pressure from outside forces such as the Philistines.

However, there were problems associated with the prospect of nationhood, including the feeling among some tribes that they were geographically isolated. At times various tribal jealousies prevented the effective welding together of the tribes into a united whole, and tribal clashes are actually recorded in Joshua 22 and Judges 12, 19, and 20.

Before the time of Saul, there had been occasional pointers to kingship, as when Gideon delivered the people (Judg. 8:22,23), but he refused the kingship. Some time later Gideon's son Abimelech tried to make himself king (Judg. 9:1–6).

Uniting factors included their common language and origin, their national adherence to the law of Moses, and the worship of Jehovah based on their unique covenant relationship with Him.

On hearing of the death of Saul, David expressed himself in an elegy (a mournful or plaintive poem) that is recognized as one of the great masterpieces of all literature. In 2 Samuel 1:21 there is a puzzling point in this elegy, on which archaeology has thrown interesting light. In the King James Version this statement is made:

> Ye mountains of Gilboa, let there be no dew, neither let there be rain upon you, nor fields of offerings. . . .

The phrase "fields of offerings" is an expression that has been a problem to Bible scholars. Now a similar passage from Canaanite poetry has been found in the excavations at Ras Shamra on the Mediterranean coast of Syria. It turns out that instead of "fields of offerings," the expression should be "upsurgings of the deep." This implies the cessation of subterranean springs of water. Thus the verse refers to dew, to rain, and to spring waters. It makes the Bible verse more readily understood, for David was telling us poetically that the very land itself should mourn, not receiving water in any form. This is another indication of the way Bible writers made use of language common at the time of their writings.[79]

This was the end of an era. Saul had been accepted

by the people. He had towered above them in physical stature. However, this giant of a man had not ventured against Goliath, the Philistine champion, even though he had been prepared to allow the youthful David to risk his life against him.

When Saul died, David became king over Judah; the one great hereditary dynasty of the Hebrew people was established. In all the divisions and strife that took place in the centuries ahead, Judah had only this Davidic dynasty, even though Israel to the north had many. The Scriptures refer to David as a "man after God's heart."

David Becomes King

The establishment of the united kingdom was not easy. David had to defeat the Philistines, and to withstand attempts against him from Ishbosheth, Saul's son, and various other opponents. He overcame his enemies and established a sound economic and military regime, and the empire was greatly extended in his time.

He was diplomat enough to realize that he needed a neutral capital, and after he had been appointed king over all twelve tribes, he chose Jerusalem as the site for the capital, this being virtually on the border between Judah and Israel. At this time Jerusalem was occupied by a Canaanite people known as Jebusites. David seized it and renamed it the city of David (2 Sam. 5:9). It has had other names through the centuries, such as "the City of Judah," "the Holy City," and "Zion."

In 2 Samuel 5:6–9 we read of the capture of Jerusalem from the Jebusites. In this account the word *tsinnor* is used. This is translated as "gutter" in the King James Version, but it is literally "watercourse" or "tunnel." The record in Scripture indicates that this watercourse was associated with the capture of the city, though it had been the boast of the Jebusite inhabitants that even the lame or the blind could defend their city.

Through the centuries, Christian scholars have taken this to refer to an entrance into the city by an underground tunnel leading up to the Pool of Siloam, believing that this was how David's men got inside. However, in modern times a problem arose: apparently the tunnel led to the Pool of Siloam, but the pool was outside the city walls in the times of David. Archaeological evidence seemed to suggest that the Bible account was wrong and that even if David's men did go along that tunnel, they would still find themselves outside the city when they got to the Pool of Siloam.

Various alternative explanations were put forward. One of these came from Albright who suggested that *tsinnor* should be translated "scaling hook," there being a similar Assyrian word with that meaning.[80] Ancient troops often used hooks to scale city walls. The explanation was plausible. Then in the 1960s new light was shed on the problem by the excavations of Kathleen Kenyon. She showed that the wall in David's time was actually farther out from the center of the city than had been previously thought. The water tunnel, which led to the Pool of Siloam was therefore well within the city.[81] Thus, once again, more complete light thrown on the Bible record has shown in still another way the reliability of the documents.

After he had captured the city, David strengthened its fortifications and eventually built himself a palace there. He also had the tabernacle reconstructed and the ark of the covenant brought to Jerusalem, and so this city became the religious center for the united tribes of Israel and Judah, as well as the national administrative center.

The historical nature of the records of David is established on other grounds as well. Earlier it had been claimed that there were not guilds of music as early as David's time, but it has been learned that both Palestine and Syria already had musicians with temple guilds such as those of Israel.[82] Many scholars had insisted on dating these Psalms of David to the times of the Maccabeans, some eight hundred years later. However, following the excavations at Ras Shamra, the Psalms attributed to David must be dated to his time. Albright writes, "To attribute such Psalms to the Maccabean period is absurd."[83]

Another interesting point on which archaeology has thrown light is the use of two titles by David — those of recorder and scribe.[84] It turns out that both these titles came directly from Egypt, the recorder being the exact Egyptian equivalent for the royal herald, and the scribe was virtually the secretary of state, the one who supervized both internal and external correspondence. Later Solomon also used an Egyptian title: "the one who is over the [royal] house." Both David and Solomon wanted the best administration possible, and if it happened that the Egyptian model was the best one to follow, that was the one they would choose.

In his time David conquered his enemies and consolidated the kingdom in a most impressive way. Solomon further consolidated and developed trade far and wide and was responsible for a great advance in building activities. However, Solomon's achievements would have been impossible without the solidified and cohesive foundation laid down in David's rule.

Chapter Notes

chapter eight

"Solomon in All His Glory"

Much of Solomon's reign has become better understood from archaeology. His building endeavors are seen in the findings at Gezer, Hazor, and Megiddo and in the temple he built with Phoenician help. Archaeology has provided the setting of the queen-of-Sheba narrative, elevating it as well to accepted history.

Solomon reigned from about 961 to 922 B.C. This period has been called the Golden Age, for the people of Israel enjoyed a new freedom from their age-old enemies. Archaeology shows some of the factors contributing to Israel's prosperity, for we now have considerable information about the surrounding nations. To the south, Egypt had been the great power through the centuries, while to the northeast, the Assyrians had been the mighty oppressors. At the time of Solomon's reign, both the Egyptians and the Assyrians were ruled by men who fell short of the stature of their predecessors. The relatively weak Tanite Dynasty controlled Egypt, while Tiglath-pileser II reigned in Assyria from about 966 to 935 B.C. The reign of Tiglath-pileser II   77 was a notoriously weak period in Assyrian history. Israel was the buffer state between these two powers, and was able to prosper, helped in no small measure by the stature and leadership of Solomon. Solomon's name means "peace," and, indeed, during the time of his reign there was no major war with any surrounding nations.

Solomon and the Phoenicians

The Phoenicians on the sea coast had considerable association with Solomon, as archaeology endorses. Solomon employed Phoenician workmen in various aspects of the temple construction, and some of the patterns given for the details of the temple are similar to those of the Phoenicians.[85] This is shown by the excavations of a number of Phoenician temples, such as the one at Hazor.

This was the time of the greatest commercial expansion the Phoenicians ever knew, and they established colonies as far west as Sardinia. They had considerable activity in mining, especially in the copper mines of Cyprus and Sardinia. Solomon also was a mining magnate, and although he was not (as previously thought) the first to engage in copper mining at Ezion-Geber on the northern tip of the Gulf of Aqabah, it is clear that he had extensive undertakings in that area. Various artifacts from his times have been recovered, including lances, spearheads, daggers, nails, and even bronze fish hooks.[86]

Solomon used state slaves, as shown in 1 Kings 9:20,21, and no doubt thousands of these people were used in his great mining activities. He also made use of forced labor from his own people, and this was a cause of considerable discontent among the freedom-loving Israelites. In fact, although Solomon was known as a man of outstanding wisdom, and the Israelites look back to this period as the golden age of their history, there were some aspects of the period that were surprising.

There was considerable unrest and discontent during his reign. His organization did not always meet with popular approval, especially when able-bodied men had to spend one month at home and two months away in Lebanon procuring cedar for his enterprises (see

The extravagant living at his royal court was another major point of criticism. Still another was that he replaced the old tribal divisions by twelve prefectures that cut across established traditions. The officers who were appointed to be in charge of these twelve divisions are listed in 1 Kings 4, and some of them were married to daughters of Solomon — thus assuring their loyalty to the crown.

Solomon maintained a large standing army, with hundreds of chariots and several thousand troops always ready for combat. This was a great safeguard against foreign aggression or interference and protected him against internal disturbances as well. Thus, although Solomon's long reign was characterized by peace, sometimes it was an uneasy peace. Nevertheless, because the nation's major expenditure was not on war, there was great national prosperity in the days of Solomon.

Another sign of peace was the great building enterprises that Solomon undertook. Many new cities were built, as the Bible indicates in 1 Kings 9, where we read of Solomon building store cities and chariot centers. Specific places referred to in that context are Gezer, Hazor, and Megiddo. Each of these cities has been excavated, and thus examples of Solomon's great building ventures have come to light, including some of his fortifications.

In 1 Kings 9:19 we read of cities that were chariot centers. This raises an interesting point about horses in the records about Solomon. We read in 1 Kings 10:28,29 that Solomon had horses imported from "Que." In the King James Version this word is translated "linen yarn," but we have learned since this translation that the word actually refers to Que in Asia Minor, a place later known as Cilicia, which became famous for its white horses. Apparently one such horse was worth four of the fast Egyptian horses. This reference in the Scriptures is another of the many pointers to the local geographic knowledge retained by the Bible writers.

Solomon's most famous building was the temple, described in 1 Kings 6. He was helped by Hiram, the **The Temple of Solomon**

The restored stables
of Solomon beneath
the temple area in
Jerusalem.

king of Tyre, who provided both materials and technical advice for the undertaking of this great enterprise. Various Phoenician temples have been excavated, and their ivory paneling and sculptures provide us with a good idea of the patterns that Solomon used. For instance, in 1 Kings 6:35 we read about cherubim, palm trees, and open flowers; and treasures such as these have been found in Phoenician temples. Archaeologists at times refer to the Phoenician temple at Hazor in Galilee—built at an earlier time than Solomon's, but with a pattern somewhat similar. However, though there are similarities to Phoenician temples, it is important to state that there is just as much resemblance to the tabernacle, constructed by the artisans of Moses during the wilderness journey. At best, the similarities to the Phoenician temples are but surface resemblances, being limited to ornamentation and physical structures. Initially there were no idolatrous statues or images of creeping things associated with the temple of God, which was to be filled only with His glory.

In comparing the temple of God with Phoenician temples we find that the differences were far greater than the similarities. The fact is that Solomon did not maintain the essential difference by recognizing only Jehovah as the true God to be worshiped. He was taking a great risk in using patterns from Phoenician temples at all, but he deviated even further when he began to recognize the gods of his various pagan wives. We again note that the writer of 1 Kings knows the associations with surrounding gods, for we read of Ashtaroth, a goddess of Sidon; Molech, a god of the Ammonites; and Chemosh, an important god of the Moabites. Shrines were built for some of these gods in Jerusalem itself (1 Kings 11:4–8). In this text, God condemns Solomon because of the introduction of foreign cults and worship.

Archaeology has thrown some light on the implements that were used in the temple. The "flesh hooks" referred to in 2 Chronicles 4:16 were actually three-pronged forks, while the "spoons" referred to in verse 22 of the same chapter were bowls or dishes, often with an open hand inscribed on the back. This explains why they were called *kaf,* the Hebrew word for "the palm of a hand." It is easy to see that the translators would think of these as "spoons," but actually they were small dishes. Possibly they were used as incense burners or for the pouring out of libations (a liquid poured out as an offering).

Two Phoenician men named Hiram are associated with Solomon, one being a highly skilled craftsman responsible for making many of the bronze implements for the temple, referred to in 1 Kings 7:13, 14. The other was the king of Tyre, referred to in 1 Kings 9:11ff.[87] He came to the Phoenician throne about 978 B.C. The latter Hiram's association with King Solomon is also referred to in the records of the Phoenicians, for a priest named Sanchuniathon wrote that King Hiram provided the ruler of Judah with building materials in exchange for the facilities of a seaport. This ancient priest tells us there were plenty of palm trees in Judah but no suitable building materials, and so Hiram had the timbers transported on eight thousand camels. We are indebted to that same Phoenician priest for additional light on a comment in 1 Kings 9:27 where we learn that Hiram sent "shipmen that had knowledge of the sea." Sanchuniathon actually gives us the names of these ancient mariners—they were Kedorus, Jaminus, and Kotilus. This is one of those interesting little points at which archaeology has added to our knowledge of particular Bible happenings.

It is relevant to point out that the Bible does not endorse the temple of Solomon (1 Chron. 28:10ff., esp. 12, 19) in the same way that it endorses the tabernacle of previous days in the wilderness. The tabernacle was devoid of much of the human factor later introduced into the building of the temple. Although God allowed His glory to fill Solomon's temple, we never read that it was made strictly according to the pattern that God had shown David by revelation, as was the case with Moses and the tabernacle (Exod. 25–31). No such *injunction* was given for the building of the temple by Solomon.

Some scholars believe that this is the reason behind the Temple Scroll, recently presented to the world by Yigael Yadin. Yadin believes the new scroll attempts to supply the "missing" Torah of God as to the specifications and measurements of the temple.[88] There was no such authoritative Torah given in the Scriptures, and it appears that an enthusiastic Hebrew teacher sought to correct what seemed to him an anomaly.

In this study we are considering the historical trustworthiness of the Bible, and one contribution of modern excavation and research has been to show that various Bible writings must be taken seriously after all. We saw that the patriarchal narratives cannot be regarded as campfire stories and that the Book of the Covenant written by Moses must be dated back to his times. Similarly, the story of the Queen of Sheba (1 Kings 10) can no longer be placed—as it had been by some scholars—in the same category as "The Arabian Nights." This is not fable or folklore, for although the actual record has not been recovered, sufficient evidence has come from archaeological research to show that this is actually a record of a literal happening at the time of Solomon. Yigael Yadin, who is a prominent Israeli archaeologist, wrote, "The substantial historicity of this event has been increasingly accepted in recent years."[89] From time to time inscriptions have been brought out from Marib, the capital of ancient Sabea (Sheba). The Sabeans used an alphabetic script that originated in Palestine. Considerable information has been gained concerning the culture, trade, and religion about the time of Solomon. There were four major spice kingdoms in the general area: Minaea, Kataban, Hadhramout, and Sheba. Sheba's capital of Marib has been partially excavated, beginning in 1951. An oval-shaped temple was recovered. It was over three hundred feet long and dedicated to the moon god, known locally as Ilumquh. The temple was beautifully laid out, with a number of water fountains.[90]

The Queen of Sheba needed Solomon's friendship, for his time coincided with a great expansion of the spice trade. Camels were increasingly utilized to cross the extensive desert area towards Solomon's seaport,

fortress, and customs center at Ezion-Geber, on the
northern tip of the Gulf of Aqabah. In 1 Kings 10 we
read of the Queen of Sheba visiting Solomon "to test
him with difficult questions," and that fits the background, for at this time there was a flowering of wisdom literature. The Hebrews, and especially Solomon,
were in the forefront of this cultural explosion. As we
read on in the chapter, we find considerable emphasis
on economic matters also, and clearly the queen was
seeking commercial advantage as well as intellectual
stimulation. Her outlets to other countries were essentially through Solomon's territory, with its series of
fortresses and customs posts extending from Jerusalem
to Ezion-Geber. The background of 1 Kings 10 comes
alive through the new knowledge about the expansion
of wisdom literature, the partial excavation of Marib,
the commercial preeminence of Solomon, and the increased capacity of the spice kingdoms to transport
their goods by camels instead of the restricted, plod-
ding donkeys previously used. With reference to his
surveys and excavation of Iron Age fortresses and
customs posts in the Negev (the south of Israel), Yo-
hanan Aharoni commented, "The story of the Queen
of Sheba is a faithful reflection of the rich trading
caravans that plied from Judah to Southern Arabia
along the highways of the Negev and the desert."[91]

Archaeological reports have added greatly to our
knowledge of the time of Solomon in such areas as
buildings, trade, and culture. Albright wrote, "The
age of Solomon was certainly one of the most flourish-
ing periods in the history of Palestine. Archaeology,
after a long silence, has finally corroborated biblical
tradition in no uncertain way."[92]

chapter nine

Assyria: The Reign of Terror

Knowledge of Assyria's history has grown rapidly. Much historical detail is known about Assyrian cities, people, customs, and monarchs. This information, especially concerning Assyria's domination of Israel, her cruel and innovative warfare, and exploits of her kings such as Shalmaneser and Sargon, has provided abundant confirmation of biblical fidelity to detail.

When Solomon died, the former general Jeroboam led a revolt of the ten northern tribes against the two tribes (Judah and Benjamin) in the south, ruled by Solomon's son Rehoboam. As a result, Solomon's kingdom was divided.

In the data we have concerning the period following Solomon's death there are many evidences of the trustworthiness of the Bible, especially in its historical details concerning the Assyrian people. However, the information is not restricted to the Assyrians. There is reference in 1 Kings 14:25 to Shishak, king of Egypt, coming against Jerusalem in the fifth year of king Rehoboam. Details about that campaign are to be found on the walls of this Pharaoh's temple at Karnak

85

in Egypt.[93] However, we will basically confine ourselves to the evidence from the Assyrian palaces.

From about 950 B.C. to the fall of Nineveh in 612 B.C. the Assyrians dominated the countries and peoples surrounding Israel and Judah. A whole series of important palaces was excavated at Nineveh and the two neighboring capitals of Nimrud and Khorsabad in the 1840s and 50s.[94] This was a very important time for the substantiation of Bible records, as well as for increased knowledge of other ancient records. Between 1837 and 1839 Major Henry Rawlinson had correctly identified the whole of the Persian alphabet from writings discovered on the Behistun Rock, which outlines some of the conquests of the Persian king, Darius the Great.[95] Armed with the new knowledge about the cuneiform inscriptions and other writings, archaeologists found it was possible to translate the masses of tablets found in some of the Assyrian palaces, especially that of Ashurbanipal from whose palace some 26,000 clay tablets were recovered beginning in 1853.[96]

The Assyrians introduced new methods of warfare and ingenious war machines that they used for siege warfare. Ashur-Nasir-Pal II, who came to the throne in Assyria in 883 B.C., was particularly responsible for a great expansion of power. He made use of battering rams, earth ramparts, ladders to scale the walls of cities, and slings to hurl stones and fire.[97] That is the background of such passages as Isaiah 10:5–11; Nahum 2:1–4; and 2 Kings 18–19. In many ways the Assyrian methods were extremely cruel; and though it seems incredible to civilized people, they kept records of the cruelties they imposed. By this means they discouraged others from daring to rise against them.

**Neighbors But
Not Friends**

It is interesting to notice that Ashur-Nasir-Pal II, who reigned from 883 to 859 B.C., was contemporary with several successive kings of Israel, including Omri, who was responsible for the building of the city of Samaria (1 Kings 16:24). On the famous Black Obelisk of Shalmaneser, Jehu is referred to as "Son of Omri."[98] Apparently Israel's neighbors referred to

Israel as "Bit Humria," which means house or land of
Omri. That is the name on the famous Moabite Stone,
which the German archaeologist F. A. Klein found
near Dhiban in 1868. It told of the rebellion of the
Moabite king Mesha against the Israelites, and pro-
vides for us a direct confirmation of the biblical story
recorded in 2 Kings 1 and 3.[99]

Another important incident relating to the Assyrian
king Shalmaneser III is the great battle of Karkat,
fought in 853 B.C., in which he defeated Israel with a
strong coalition that included thousands of Assyrians,
their chariots, and their cavalry. He boasts that among
those he defeated were "ten thousand foot soldiers of
Ahab the Israelite," and that the very valleys flowed
with the blood of his victims.[100]

We referred above to the "Black Obelisk of Shalmaneser." On it King Jehu is pictured prostrate before
Shalmaneser, paying him tribute.[101] Those who remember Jehu will remember him as the furious chariot
driver (a man ahead of his times!), but he is also
famous because he is the only king of Israel depicted in
stone in this way. The person actually "pictured"
might be his emissary, paying the tribute on Jehu's
behalf.

This particular incident is not recorded in Scripture,
illustrating the fact that often archaeology adds to our
knowledge of the incidents, customs, and people recorded in the Bible.

These Assyrian people disappeared from history
after defeat by Nebuchadnezzar in the battle of Carchemish in 605 B.C., and yet the Bible writers knew
many details about them, even recording the names
of their kings in proper chronological sequence.
Likewise, the Assyrians referred to the Bible kings
quite accurately.

The evidence of eyewitness reporting in the Bible
records is very strong. It would be a suitable archaeological activity, using recovered Assyrian records, to go back through these records and identify
which kings were reigning at particular periods of
time. But the Bible writers casually—yet always
correctly—referred to Assyrian kings by name, always in the right time periods. As we go through the

Bible records, we read of such kings as Tiglath-pileser, Shalmaneser, Sargon, Sennacherib, and Esarhaddon, all in correct chronological sequence. The rulers of other nations are also brought in at appropriate points, providing us with the synchronizations touching on the Egyptians, the Israelites, the people of Judah, and the Syrians, as well as others.

In addition, various other kings of Israel are mentioned in the Assyrian records. In 2 Kings 15:19,20 we learn that Israel's King Menahem paid Tiglath-pileser a thousand talents of silver as tribute, and this payment is referred to in Tiglath-pileser's records also.[102] Menahem himself levied a tax of fifty shekels each on all the mighty men of wealth, and we now know that this was the approximate price of an able-bodied slave at that time. The Israelites were virtually redeeming themselves, instead of being bought as slaves.

Skepticism Reversed

It is interesting that in 1 Chronicles 5:26 we read that God stirred up the spirit of Tiglath-pileser, king of Assyria, but he is also referred to there by the name Pul. At first this seems to be a mistake; then we look again and notice that a singular verb is used in association with the two names. It turns out that Pullu was the throne name adopted by Tiglath-pileser when he became king of Babylon. He took this Babylonian name to avoid giving offense to the Babylonian people. The casual Bible reference is a remarkable piece of local color, and it is this sort of evidence that consistently reminds us that the Bible prophets and recorders lived against the backgrounds claimed for them. They confidently referred to kings and customs of the people with whom they and their leaders were in direct contact.

One of the most interesting confirmations of this general time period relates to the Assyrian king Sargon, referred to by name only in Isaiah 20:1. There we read that Sargon, the king of Assyria, sent his "tartan" (commander-in-chief) against the Philistine city of Ashdod, on the Mediterranean coast. Many Bible critics believed that this was clearly a mistake, for no King Sargon was known. Perhaps the reader can

Assyria: The
Reign of Terror

*Relief of Sargon II,
the conqueror of Sa-
maria, found at Khor-
sabad palace.*

capture a bit of the excessively skeptical spirit in which such a reference would be dismissed simply because it is stated nowhere else. It was learnedly argued that King Shalmaneser must be meant, until Sargon's huge palace at Khorsabad was discovered. Not only that, but a wall description was found of the very battle referred to in Isaiah 20.[103] Many years later there came further confirmation when the city of Ashdod was excavated. Archaeologists found three pieces of a broken memorial stele that turned out to be the boasting of Sargon about his capture and defeat of this Philistine city.

The Bible reference was substantiated and in fact demonstrated the reliability of the Bible in no less than three different ways. It showed that there was a King Sargon, despite those critics who insisted there was no such king. Second, it confirmed the particular reference to a campaign by Sargon against Philistine Ashdod. Third, it showed that the Bible writers even knew the titles of the Assyrians with whom they were in frequent (though hostile) contact. Prophets such as Isaiah and Jeremiah confidently and always correctly used such titles as Tartan, Rabshakeh (chief officer), Rabsaris (chief treasurer), and Tupsarru (captain).[104] Critics are frequently claiming that biblical texts are later than the dates the texts give for themselves. Yet, in spite of the fact that the Assyrians disappeared from history after the Battle of Carchemish in 605 B.C., these Bible writers even knew such intimate details as the titles of the enemy.

Let's change contexts for a moment. Who would know the titles of army officers in World War II, or in the wars fought in Korea or Vietnam? Only those who had been in those conflicts or who had direct contact with those who had been there. The way these Bible writers confidently and consistently use the titles of the enemy is a clear pointer to the fact that they were writing against the backgrounds claimed for them by the Bible.

It is highly significant that those same Bible writers not only wrote history, but they penned their remarkable prophecies as well. They pinpointed the very city

where Jesus would be born (Mic. 5:2), that He would
be born to a virgin mother (Isa. 7:14), the time of His
official presentation to Israel as the promised Messiah
(Dan. 9:25), that He would be betrayed by a friend (Ps.
41:9), sold for thirty pieces of silver (Zech. 11:12),
would die by crucifixion (Zech. 12:10), be buried with
the rich (Isa. 53:9), and would rise again from the dead
(Ps. 16:10).

We do not know for sure which Assyrian king took
the people of Israel into captivity. At that point the
Bible writer simply refers to "the king of Assyria," as
though he was unsure who the king was, and that might
well have been the case. Shalmaneser V died about
that time, possibly at the very time when Samaria was
besieged, and one of his generals (possibly his son)
became king and took to himself the name of a great
predecessor, King Sargon of ancient Akkad. This was
the new king referred to above, as we see in Isaiah
20:1.

Israel Falls Captive to Assyria

Years later Sargon himself boasted that he had taken
27,290 of the Israelites captive, but Assyrian kings
were seldom known for their humility, and it is possible that this boast simply reflected the Assyrian practice of claiming a major victory for every year of the
king's reign.[105] It is possible that Sargon simply carried out the "mopping-up" operations after Shalmaneser had been successful against the Israelites.
However it happened, it is certain that in 722/721 B.C.
the Israelites were carried into captivity as a nation,
and to a great extent their identity was lost because of
the Assyrian policy of mixing their captive peoples
with others of different nationality and tongue. This
shrewd policy minimized the chances of rising against
the Assyrian overlords.

While the ten tribes of Israel were taken captive in
722/721 B.C., Judah to the south struggled on for over
a century, but she too had great problems with the
Assyrians. Sennacherib is especially pertinent because
of his contacts with the people of Judah, and details of
his campaigns are referred to in 2 Kings 18–19, 2

Sennacherib Frustrated at Jerusalem

Rocks, Relics,
and Biblical
Reliability

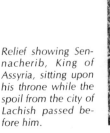

Relief showing Sennacherib, King of Assyria, sitting upon his throne while the spoil from the city of Lachish passed before him.

Chronicles 32, and Isaiah 36–37. He destroyed many of the fenced cities of Judah, and a common fix of the Bible and archaeology is when the defeated Hezekiah, king of Judah, agreed to pay tribute to Sennacherib, sending it to him at the city of Lachish. This payment of tribute is recorded in the records of the Bible (2 Kings 18:13–15) and in the annals of Sennacherib.

There is an interesting record about Sennacherib relating to his siege of Jerusalem. At that time King Hezekiah was assured by the prophet Isaiah that not so much as an arrow would be shot into the city (Isa. 37:33). Such was the case, for exactly as the Bible records, thousands of Sennacherib's troops died at the time they besieged Jerusalem, and the rest of his troops withdrew. Unable to boast of this as a great victory, Sennacherib "messaged" the story a bit and recorded the following in his annals: "As for Hezekiah the Jew, who did not submit to my yoke, forty-six of his strong-walled cities, as well as the small cities in their neighborhood, which were without number, . . . I besieged and took . . . himself, like a caged bird, I shut up in Jerusalem, his Royal City. . . ."[106]

Both the Bible and the records of Sennacherib make it clear that tribute was sent after Sennacherib to the city of Lachish in southern Judah, but it is nevertheless a fact that Sennacherib could not destroy Jerusalem.

Denied a victory at the capital of these troublesome people of Judah, he made the best of a bad job by boasting that he had shut up their king like a bird in a cage. As we examine these two records from the opposite perspectives of these people, we realize that here we have a direct point of confirmation.

About that same time Hezekiah showed the treasures of Judah to the Babylonian king Merodach-Baladan, and the prophet Isaiah reproved King Hezekiah for his folly (2 Kings 20). The records of Sennacherib about this Merodach-Baladan are fairly extensive. Sennacherib refers to the Babylonian as "an instigator of revolt, a plotter of rebellion, a doer of evil whose guilt is heavy."[107] Merodach-Baladan didn't disappoint Sennacherib. He proved to be a schemer right through his life—setting people against people, pointing to his own greatness even when others were responsible for the activities of which he boasted, and in various ways fitting Sennacherib's description of him as a man whose "heart is wicked." Little wonder that Isaiah the prophet rebuked the king of Judah for being prepared to make an ally of this infamous schemer! Isaiah was a man of discernment, and his assessment of Merodach-Baladan's character was an accurate one. Eventually Sennacherib was killed by two of his own sons, as related in Isaiah 37:38, 2 Kings 19:37, and 2 Chronicles 32:21. The same story is told in the records of Sennacherib's successor, his son Esarhaddon.[108] Thus it is clear from both the Bible and the Assyrian records that he was the next king of Assyria. The biblical records were written by men who were alive at the time, able to grasp important facts of history and put them down factually and consistently. It seems impossible to shake the impression that these biblical passages are history of the highest integrity. Esarhaddon tells of the incident of the killing of his father as follows:

> A firm determination fell upon my brothers. They forsook the gods and turned to their deeds of violence, plotting evil. . . . Evil words and deeds contrary to the will of the gods they perpetrated against me. Unholy hostility they planned behind my back.

My brothers . . . trusting in their own counsel . . . committed unwarranted acts. . . . To gain the kingship, they slew Sennacherib their father.[109]

Archaeology further elaborates our knowledge of these times. The famous Ashurbanipal collected many ancient records, from which we learn that when he became king he had his uncles brought back from exile and executed in the very temple where they had killed their father.[110] Often the points given by biblical authors seem to be insignificant, but we who live millennia after the events have been able to see from archaeological evidence that frequently those seemingly insignificant details are important in validating historical truth.

**Manasseh,
King of Judah**

In Judah, King Hezekiah was followed by his wicked son, Manasseh. This wickedness is clearly portrayed in the Bible at such places as 2 Kings 21. Here we read of magic, astrology, and enchantments, fitting in with the current picture of background information from archaeology. From this time there is a mass of tablets that speak of magic, divination, and astrology in Judah. A flood of idolatrous and superstitious practices is recorded, and they fit the biblical background shown for King Manasseh exactly. He is also known in Assyrian records, identified there as a king who provided building materials for a palace for the Assyrian king Esarhaddon, referred to earlier. He is also listed as paying tribute to Esarhaddon's son, Ashurbanipal.

The Assyrians eventually fell before the might of the Chaldeans, who combined with the Medes, and the Chaldean monarch Nabopolasser was established as king. It was Nebuchadnezzar, the son of Nabopolasser and a general in his army, who was responsible for the ultimate great victory in 605 B.C. at Carchemish, where the final remnants of the Assyrian army were defeated. In that same year Nebuchadnezzar himself became king and was to be an outstanding ruler of Babylon.

The Exile in Babylon

Once-held theories that biblical stories of the exile in Babylon were pious forgery, written centuries after the period they claimed for themselves, have been overturned. Evidences from tablets found in Babylon's famous Hanging Gardens, linguistic evidences, historical accuracies brought to light by finds such as the Cyrus Cylinder have restored the highest confidence in Ezra, Nehemiah, Ezekiel, Daniel, and Jeremiah.

When the people of Judah eventually were carried into captivity by the Babylonians under Nebuchadnezzar, the prophet Jeremiah wrote them a famous letter (in chapter 29 of his prophecy), stating that after seventy years the people would return and settle again in their own land. This was literally fulfilled.

One of the interesting things about the Exile is that the Jewish people still recognized their king Jehoiachin as king, even though he was in captivity also. About three hundred tablets, dating to between 597 and 570 B.C., were found in the famous Hanging Gardens of Babylon, and among them was a reference to the fact that Jehoiachin and his five sons were being given

Rocks, Relics,
and Biblical
Reliability

A Babylonian tablet
relating Nebuchad-
nezzar's invasion of
Judah and the siege
and surrender of
Jerusalem.

monthly rations.[111] The tablets also included the
names of the sons of Aga, the king of Ashkelon, who is
referred to in Jeremiah 47:5–7.

Apparently Judah's king was treated well. This was
a point of political expediency by the Babylonians to
ensure that he "behaved" himself while they held him
hostage. The Bible itself says (2 Kings 25:27–30) that
Jehoiachin was still being treated well by the Babylonians thirty-seven years after his own captivity.

Albright has written extensively about the exile of
the Jews and their return. At times he shows how
dramatically different are scholarly opinions today,
compared with what they were in the writings of earlier
critics. He tells of the attacks against the authenticity of
this period of Old Testament history, especially at the
end of the last century. The writings of Ezra,
Nehemiah, Ezekiel, Jeremiah, and various other
prophets were virtually put to one side. The views of
such scholars have been categorically disproved by the

Albright tells us, "It is now possible, thanks to archaeological discoveries, to reconstruct the situation of the Jews in Palestine during the Exile with general clarity," and "All internal and linguistic objections to dating the final redaction of the Chronicler's work after the early fourth century have been disproved by recent archaeological research."[112]

In a survey such as this it is not our purpose to elaborate on those remarkable prophecies about the cities of Nineveh, Babylon, and Tyre, but it should be noted that the genuineness of the prophetic writings again becomes clear when we consider such prophecies. The fact that the prophecies are genuine shows that the basic writings in which they are set are also genuine. There are specific points that, when added together, demonstrate the remarkable nature of these prophecies with their fulfillments of history. Nineveh did become a place for sheep to graze on and for the herds of the nation to wander across, even as Zephaniah had declared (Zeph. 2:14); and the opposite prophecy about Babylon being a place where the shepherd would *not* graze his sheep (Isa. 13:20) was also literally fulfilled (and is to this day!).

Similarly, Nebuchadnezzar and Alexander the Great, separated by over two centuries, nevertheless "cooperated" to ensure that the divine prophecies were minutely fulfilled in relation to the city of Tyre. The stones, the timber, and the dust of Tyre *were* cast into the sea, as foretold by Ezekiel in 26:12, when Alexander used them to build a great causeway to link the mainland city to the island, and "great water" certainly did cover these ruins. Thus it became part of the "place for the spreading of nets" (Ezek. 26:14).

The Rise of Daniel in Babylon

Close to the end of the Babylonian captivity, we have the story of Daniel who became "third in the kingdom" (Dan. 5:29). The Babylonian king named in the Bible was Belshazzar. For many years some scholars thought this was an error, for no King Belshazzar was known. Nabonidus was recognized as the last king of Babylon before the troops of the Medes and the Persians captured his city, until the famous Nabonidus Chronicle was found. It showed that Nabonidus appointed his son Belshazzar as king while he was absent over a period of several years from his capital city of Babylon.[113] Other helpful documents have also been found. One of them shows that Nabonidus contacted his son from Tema in Arabia, with specific instructions that Belshazzar obeyed.

Nabonidus also stated that he had entrusted *sarrulam* (kingship) to his eldest son. Thus when we read of Daniel being promised the place of "third in the kingdom," we are witnessing a remarkable piece of eyewitness recording. Technically, Nabonidus was still number one, his son Belshazzar was the coregent and so number two, and Daniel was to become number three.

There are other evidences of eyewitness recording by Daniel. That he knew Nebuchadnezzar rebuilt Babylon (Dan. 4:30) is a problem by those who argue for a late date for Daniel. This fact of history was recovered by excavation only in modern times, yet Daniel had recorded it correctly. One critic wrote that this was a difficulty, the answer to which "we shall presumably never know."[114] Those who argue for Daniel to be dated to the Maccabean period have a problem explaining this piece of eyewitness recording. Linguistic pointers from the Dead Sea Scrolls (e.g., a recent targum of Job) also suggest an early, not a late, date for Daniel. The early date is traditionally believed by the Jews, and the Bible so claims (Dan. 1:1–6). The references to magic, astrology, and soothsayers (Dan. 1:20; 2:10; 4:7; 5:7, et al.) are all pointers to the time of Nebuchadnezzar. Excavation has produced considerable information about magic and divination, about which Daniel had detailed knowledge. This again points to an early date.

Cyrus and the End of the Exile

The overthrow of the nonhistorical view of the Exile and the return of the Jews came with the finding of the famous Cyrus Cylinder, in which Cyrus, king of Persia, tells how the Babylonian god Marduk had instructed him to restore rightful worship

*The Cyrus Cylinder,
which records the
decree of King Cyrus
of Persia, established
the historicity of the
exile and the return of
the Hebrews from
Babylon.*

in Babylon.[115] The same story is told from the Hebrew point of view in the last chapter of 2 Chronicles and again in Ezra 1:1–4. When we allow for the perspective of the people of Cyrus as against that of the Hebrews, the two records agree remarkably well. Apparently there were a number of copies of this "Cyrus Decree," each varying according to the peoples who were specifically addressed. By this decree the Hebrew people were given leave to rebuild the temple in Jerusalem. In the eye of Scripture, Cyrus was merely the instrument of God, used to fulfill His purposes. He was dramatically different from his predecessors and had remarkable ideas of personal freedom.

The Jewish Exile thus came to an end after seventy years, just as Jeremiah had predicted in two different places (Jer. 25; 29). A large number of the Jewish people returned to their own land to worship the Lord in the appointed way, and the prophecy was fulfilled in remarkable detail.

The same can be said about the style of writing of the Book of Ezra, for as Albright says, "If we turn to the Book of Ezra, recent discoveries have indicated the authenticity of its official documents in the most striking way." Albright shows that the language of Ezra had been seriously challenged, but that some of the very words that have been challenged have turned up in Egyptian, Aramaic, and Babylonian cuneiform documents that date to the exact time of Ezra. Albright goes on: "If it were practicable to quote from still unpublished Aramaic documents from fifth century Egypt, the weight of factual evidence would crush all opposition."[116]

Ezra was a careful historian, a fact that is tremendously important when we recognize that he is credited with the bringing together of the books of the Old Testament and that they were virtually the same as they are in modern times (though the arrangement of the books is sometimes different).

In this period of biblical reporting, as with earlier periods, there have been points previously criticized but now known to bear the mark of authentic reporting. One example relates to Geshem the Arab who is referred to in Nehemiah 2:19; 6:2,6.[117] This man is now known from two other sources, one being a series of inscriptions near ancient Dedan, a desert area east of Palestine. He is also referred to on a silver bowl found in an Arab temple on the Egyptian border; the bowl was dedicated to a goddess by a son of Geshem.[118]

Once it was thought that Sanballat, the governor of Samaria, lived at a considerably later time than Nehemiah and that this indicated that Nehemiah's writing dated after the time claimed for him in the Bible. Now we know that the Bible record is accurate. "Sanballat" turns out to be a name that was used at least three times in periods of history covering several generations.[119] Once again, archaeological research has demonstrated that the Bible was right after all. The fact is, the Bible records of history must be taken seriously.

Still another convincing evidence of the genuineness of the Bible records is in *The Mysterious Numbers of the Hebrew Kings,* by Edwin R. Thiele.[120] Where once it seemed that the dates of the kings in the divided-kingdom period were inaccurate and vague, he has been able to show remarkable synchronisms and, as he states, "We are now in a position to construct an edifice of Hebrew history chronologically sound in the area of the Kingdoms of Israel and Judah." Thiele goes on to say that in his book "are found the links of a chain of chronological evidence extending from Rehoboam to Hezekiah in Judah, and from Jeroboam to Hoshea in Israel, with the reigns of both nations constantly interwoven with each other in strict accord with requirements of the data provided by the original Hebrew recorders, and all now bound together in a completed chain without a missing link."[121]

Once again, an area that many believed was total confusion has been shown to be staggeringly accurate recording, with fine chronological interweaving that cannot be claimed for any other book of ancient history.

Chapter Notes

chapter eleven

The Dead Sea Scrolls

The impact of the Dead Sea Scrolls has been enormous. The quality of manuscript evidence has been vastly improved, as Dead Sea copies of the Old Testament books predated the earliest copies otherwise known by a thousand years. A comparison of the two revealed the great care exercised in the transmission process. Conservative views of Isaiah's prophecies were strengthened. The background and date of John's Gospel were clarified, as idioms and teachings previously said to have been Hellenistic (and therefore remote from the life of Jesus) were shown to be Judean instead.

The story of the Dead Sea Scrolls is now widely known. Fragments of biblical and other documents have been found at various places in the general vicinity of the Dead Sea, especially at Qumran, Marabba'at, and Masada. Easily the most significant for the findings of scrolls is Qumran, where the scrolls were hidden in almost inaccessible caves as the community's monastic headquarters were being attacked.

Parts of every book of the Old Testament except Esther have been found among the scrolls, and it is probable that Esther's absence is merely accidental. It 103 is known that the Bedouin people actually found many of the writings long before 1947 when the modern world heard of them and that they burned many of them because of the fragrant aroma they gave off. Who knows how many scrolls of Esther and other books of the Bible were destroyed around Bedouin campfires over the last two thousand years?

This is not the place to discuss the finding of various secular scrolls such as the *Manual of Discipline,* the *War of the Sons of Light With the Sons of Darkness,* the *Genesis Apocryphon,* the *Collection of Thanksgiving Psalms,* the *Copper Scroll* (which proved to be a treasure map), or even the more recently recovered *Temple Scroll,* which is twenty-eight feet in length.[122] Nor do we propose to discuss in detail the evidences of the search for the Messiah, except to say, briefly, that these people at Qumran could not reconcile Old Testament Scriptures such as Deuteronomy 18:18 (a prophet like Moses) and Isaiah 11:1 (a Davidic Messiah) with Genesis 49:10 (where the rule of Israel is linked with Judah). "David their king" is also linked with sacrifice in Hosea 3:4,5. "The Qumran community expected that life would continue as it was until the coming of a prophet and the anointed ones (messiahs) of Aaron and Israel."[123] This indicates that they were looking for a messianic prophet, another one who would be a messianic priest, and still another who would reign as a messianic king. One document from Cave 4 at Qumran was a collection of messianic passages from the Old Testament, including Deuteronomy 18:18,19 (referring to a prophet); Numbers 24:15–17 (referring to a king); and Deuteronomy 33:8–11 (where Moses pronounced blessings on the priestly tribe of Levi).[124]

Further fragments from Qumran, more recently recovered, refer to Melchizedek, known in the Bible only at Genesis 14, Psalm 110, and Hebrews 5 and 7. He was king of Salem and priest of the Most High God (Gen. 14:18.* In these late Qumran fragments

---

*"Salem" has traditionally been linked with Jerusalem; but at a public lecture at the University of Michigan in November 1976, Professor Pettinato (epigrapher—translator of the now-famous

Melchizedek is associated with a series of messianic quotations, including Leviticus 25 (God's judgment) and Isaiah 52 (the herald proclaiming salvation).[125]

Putting these facts together, we find that the Qumran community apparently was searching for at least two messiahs (a Davidic king and an Aaronic priest), and possibly another two (a prophet like Moses and another priest figure like Melchizedek). This would mean the expectation of possibly four messiahs in all. Other intertestamental writings (between the Old and New Testaments) appear to support this search for more than one messiah, e.g., the *Testaments of the Twelve Patriarchs*.[126]

The New Testament writers saw in Jesus the fulfillment of the messianic prophecies. He was David's son (Matt. 1:1), the great prophet who was the very Word of God (John 1:1,14–21), the good shepherd who would offer Himself as the Lamb of God (John 10:14,15; 1:29), and the eternal high priest after the order of Melchizedek (Heb. 5:6–10).

He was also the fulfillment of Isaiah's messianic prophecies, and this becomes clear when we compare Isaiah 53:7,8 with Acts 8:32–35. In that passage of Acts we read of Philip the evangelist showing Jesus as the fulfillment of the passage about the suffering Servant. The Ethiopian eunuch was reading it aloud as he traveled along in his chariot, and Philip elaborated on that passage to him.

A Giant Step in Manuscript Evidence

The discovery of the Dead Sea Scrolls brought an immeasurably greater quality of manuscript evidence. It meant that scholars now have copies of much of the Old Testament in Hebrew, dating approximately one thousand years earlier than the earliest Hebrew Old Testament texts previously possessed.[127] There were several textual traditions recovered in the scrolls from Qumran, and these included both Massoretic and Septuagint (LXX) texts.[128] It was surprising to find how relatively insignificant were the variations from the accepted text. By comparative studies it has been

---

Ebla-Tell Mardikh texts) announced that both Salem and Jerusalem were known in trade documents.

shown that in some places the Dead Sea Scrolls in Hebrew were inferior to the texts behind the Septuagint (Greek) version of the Old Testament. That is not as surprising as it might at first seem, for it is traditionally believed that when the Septuagint version was undertaken in the third century, B.C., seventy-two of the best available Jewish scholars were chosen for that important work of translation. The scribes at Qumran would not necessarily have had that same standard of scholarship.

The scrolls have cleared up a few points where there was confusion, but not one aspect of doctrine has been affected by these important manuscript findings. There is a phrase in Isaiah 21:8 that reads in the King James Version: "And he cried, a lion. . . ." This should be amended to read, "And he who saw cried, 'My Lord!'" The word *lion* should read "he who saw," this stemming from only a slight change in the vowels. The original Hebrew had no vowels, and so a mistranslation such as this is easily understood.

One interesting problem now resolved relates to the address of Stephen in Acts 7:14 where he refers to an incident recorded in Genesis 46:26,27. The Dead Sea Scrolls texts show that the Genesis texts probably should read "three score and fifteen," just as it is in Stephen's address, and not "seventy people" as it is in the King James Version. The text behind the King James Version had apparently become corrupted at this point.

Another interesting point of reference to the Old Testament is that John the Baptist refers to himself as "a voice crying in the wilderness" (Isa. 40:3; cf. Mark 1:3). This quotation was a favorite one for the Qumran community, for they regarded themselves as the communal embodiment of that "voice crying in the wilderness." Possibly John was correcting their false conception, for we read that he lived in the general area of the Dead Sea for some time before his public presentation to his own people. Whatever the explanation, the fact is that John was quoting from the Old Testament Scriptures and relating that prophecy to himself. This certainly is in harmony with Old Testament prophecies, for the Messiah was to have a herald before his appearance, and John fulfilled those prophecies completely.

One of the most important implications of the Dead Sea Scrolls to Old Testament studies is that it can no longer be argued that the prophecy of Isaiah should be dated after the time of Jesus, as some severe critics had claimed. Of course, the very fact that they took this extreme position is indicative of the force of the prophetic testimony. A number of copies of Isaiah's prophecies have been found, and indeed one of the very first manuscripts brought out by Mahommed El Dhib (Mahommed the Wolf) was a scroll of Isaiah, twenty-four feet in length.

The twenty-four-foot scroll of Isaiah found at Qumran opened to columns 32–33 (Isaiah 38:8–40:28).

It had been popular for some time to say that not one but two prophets were brought together in the Book of Isaiah. This is the Deutero-Isaiah theory. Interestingly enough, we found no break between Isaiah chapters 39 and 40 of this Dead Sea text, though a break might have been expected if there were two great prophets brought together under the name of Isaiah. There is a squiggle in the margin, but it was a common practice to make such a mark when one wished to draw attention to something in the text. The break that many scholars had anticipated was nowhere to be found. Even if the original Scroll of Isaiah were dated only to the second century B.C., the widely accepted date for the making of this particular copy, it would be no less remarkable to find in it a series of prophecies about the Messiah that were so completely fulfilled in the person of Jesus Christ. However, the Qumran Scroll was itself but a copy of earlier copies, and the evidence is that the original of Isaiah must have dated to a considerably earlier time than that of the Qumran community. The prophecies of Isaiah about the Messiah are again established as genuine by the findings of these manuscripts.

Qumran and the New Testament

There are similarities to the New Testament as well. One of the most important points of similarity is that both the Scrolls and the New Testament reach back for their roots into the Old Testament. This is not surprising, for the Qumran community was Jewish, Jesus was Jewish, and His early disciples also were Jewish.

In *That Incredible Book the Bible*[129] we outline a number of the points of similarity between the Qumran community and New Testament teachings. In Matthew 18:15 the procedure for dealing with a brother who is in error is outlined: he is to be personally reproved, and, if necessary, witnesses are to be called. Only after that has failed to bring a satisfactory result is the matter to be brought before the assembly. The community members at Qumran were also admonished not to reprove one of their community in anger, nor to bring one of their members before the assembled community until he first had been dealt with before witnesses.

In fact, the similarities between the practices of the Qumran community and New Testament teachings are substantial enough that some scholars have said Jesus and His followers had merely borrowed from the Essenes at Qumran.[130] The Qumran community had a teacher plus twelve disciples, they had goods in common, they practiced baptism daily, and they shared a communal meal. These are some of the practices that are supposed to be similar to those in the New Testament, but in fact none of them shows any distinctive association with the New Testament. The idea of "the twelve" goes back to the Old Testament with the twelve patriarchs and twelve tribes, and although the voluntary sharing of goods is referred to in Acts 4:32, this was not the same practice that was arbitrarily enforced at Qumran. There a person who joined the community handed over his goods and did not get them back even if he departed. Nor was baptism the same rite as that of the New Testament, for at Qumran it was a daily rite, part of the regular ritual. Other Jewish people also practiced baptism, but for the New Testament Christian after the resurrection of Christ, baptism was a symbol of association with His death, burial, and resurrection. It spoke of newness of life, even though the believer might be treated as dead by the world.

Jesus and the Teacher of Righteousness

Exaggerated claims have been made at times about the figure of Qumran literature, the Teacher of Righteousness himself; conjectures have even been made that this was the original of the Great Teacher of the New Testament. This is totally without validity, and there is *no evidence whatever* that the Teacher of Righteousness was crucified or rose again, as has sometimes been claimed. A. Dupont-Summer is frequently quoted to the effect that the Teacher of Righteousness was tortured and murdered, then "after his earthly career and his ignominious death, he is now to be translated to an eschatological plane, invested with full messianic glory, and enthroned as chief of the universe."[131] W. S. Lasor shows that others have expanded this teaching, "to the consternation of many sincere Christians," but "the simple fact is that scholars of all shades of theological presuppositions, or of none at all (if that be possible), have differed with Dupont-Summer's conclusions."[132] The Teacher of Righteousness cannot be identified with Jesus Christ.

The title "Teacher of Righteousness" was simply that, and it seems that there would have been successive people who took that title. Also the Teacher of Righteousness himself looked on to the coming of the Messiah and never claimed to be the Messiah. Jesus made it clear that He was that Messiah (Matt. 16:16,17,20; 22:42–45; 23:8,10; 24:5); He even sat by a well in Samaria and told a woman who came there that He was the Messiah (John 4:26).

Another significant conclusion that may be drawn

from the Dead Sea Scrolls bears on the date and background of John's Gospel. Many scholars have reacted to Jesus' claims to deity so evident throughout this Gospel, and have sought to date it as late as possible, so that time for Hellenistic (Greek) influences on the original story might be had. However, the Dead Sea Scrolls have made it evident that the background to John's Gospel is Judean, not Hellenistic. John uses parallels like "light and darkness," "truth and perversity," and other expressions such as "sons of light," "brotherly love," and "fountain of living water"— all of which were Jewish expressions, common to both John and Qumran.

The Dead Sea Scrolls have made it clear that the writings of John were set in the context claimed for them in the New Testament and not at some considerably later time, nor by a non-Jewish writer. They have the imprint of authenticity.

The Dead Sea Scrolls have also thrown light on various words and phrases in the New Testament, one especially interesting example being the expression "because of the angels" in 1 Corinthians 11:10. In the battle against the forces of evil, we read in the War Scroll of the Qumran community, that the soldiers were to be pure, "because of the angels who accompany the troops." Thus the Dead Sea Scrolls have thrown light on Paul's statement, making it clear that the angels could not help human forces if they themselves were offended by human impurity.

Material about the Dead Sea Scrolls continues to be published, and there is a great deal of work yet to be undertaken. There seems little doubt that the next decade will throw even more light on the biblical text as the work of identifying and translating the Scrolls continues, leading to eventual publication.

chapter twelve

Archaeology
and the
New Testament

The work of Sir William Ramsey and others has shown the remarkable accuracy of Luke's recording and his intimate knowledge of local customs, terms, and attitudes. Recovered papyri documents enrich our understanding of New Testament words and teachings. In all, archaeology has made significant comment on the extraordinary quality of both the Gospels and the Epistles as source materials for their times.

A number of good books are available relating to the archaeology of the New Testament, and one of the best is a small booklet entitled *Luke the Historian* by J. A. Thompson. He was the author's predecessor as Director of the Australian Institute of Archaeology, holding the position when the author first joined as a lecturer in the early 1950s.

Thompson surveyed and analyzed some of the major evidence, especially from the findings of Sir William Ramsay who says of himself:

I may fairly claim to have entered on this investigation without any prejudice in favour of the conclusion which I shall now attempt to justify to the reader. On the contrary, I began with a mind unfavourable to it, for the ingenuity and apparent completeness of the Tubingen theory had at one time quite convinced me. It did not lie then in my line of life to investigate the subject minutely; but more recently I found myself often brought in contact with the Book of Acts as an authority for the topography, antiquities and society of Asia Minor. It was gradually borne in upon me that in various details the narrative showed marvellous truth. In fact, beginning with the fixed idea that the work was essentially a second-century composition, and never relying on its evidence as trustworthy for first-century conditions, I gradually came to find it a useful ally in some obscure and difficult investigations. [133]

Thompson analyzes Ramsay's conclusions under various headings, and basically they are as follows: Luke demonstrated a remarkably accurate knowledge of geographical and political ideas. He referred correctly to provinces that were established at that time, as indicated in Acts 15:41; 16:2,6–8. He identified regions, such as that referred to in Acts 13:49, and various cities, as in Acts 14:6. He demonstrated a clear knowledge of local customs, such as those relating to the speech of the Lycaonians (Acts 14:11), some aspects relating to the foreign woman who was converted at Athens (Acts 17:34), and he even knew that the city of Ephesus was known as "the temple-keeper of Artemis" (Acts 19:35).

Throughout the Bible, one of the clearest evidences that the writers understood the background of the times is that they referred to the customs of various officials with great precision. This sort of accuracy is seen in Luke, for he refers to different local officers by their exact titles—the proconsul (deputy) of Cyprus (Acts 13:7), the magistrates at Philippi (Acts 16:20,35), the politarchs (another word for magistrates) at Thessalonica (Acts 17:6), the proconsul of Achaia (Acts 18:12), and the treasurer at Corinth (Aedile)—which was the title of the man known as Erastus at Corinth (Acts 19:22; Rom. 16:23). There were "certain chiefs," referring to heads of imperial, political, and religious organizations (Acts 19:31). In that same context we read of the town clerk and the temple-keeper at Ephesus (Acts 19:35 RSV) and there was also the "chief man" (the Roman governor) at Malta (Acts 28:7).

Luke had accurate knowledge about various local events such as the famine in the days of Claudius Caesar (Acts 11:29); he was aware that Zeus and Hermes were worshiped together at Lystra, though this was unknown to modern historians (Acts 14:11,12). He knew that Diana or Artemis was especially the goddess of the Ephesians (Acts 19:28); and he was able to describe the trade at Ephesus in religious images (Acts 19:26,27). Obviously he knew a great deal about local buildings and areas, referring confidently and yet casually to the marketplace at Philippi (Acts 16:19); to the gate and river at Philippi (Acts 16:13); to the marketplace at Athens (Acts 17:17); to the Areopagus at Athens (Acts 17:19,22); to the marketplace at Corinth, which was the place of judgment (Acts 18:12); to the theater at Ephesus (Acts 19:29); and to the temple of the great goddess at Ephesus (Acts 19:27).

The theater at Ephesus, mentioned by Luke in Acts 19:29.

At all of these points, archaeology has had something significant to say, sometimes where the biblical record had previously seemed to be in error. One good example relates to those magistrates at Philippi. In Acts 16:20,35 we read of the magistrates being referred to as "praetors." Strictly, their title should have been *duumvir*, but it was as though they called themselves "senior magistrates" instead of "magistrates." Ramsay showed by an inscription recovered in another Roman colony, Capua, that Cicero had spoken of the magistrates: "Although they are called duumvirs in the other colonies, these men wish to be called praetors."[134]

This is a point at which critics had thought Luke was in error, but the fact is Luke was better informed than those who opposed him. His writings constantly bear this impress of authenticity. He was an eyewitness of so much that is recorded in the Acts, and the source documents have now been recognized as first-class historical writings. It is little wonder that Ramsay eventually became a devout follower of Christ as a direct result of his archaeological research. He came to recognize just how fine a historian Luke was and eventually wrote, "The present writer takes the view that Luke's history is unsurpassed in respect of its trustworthiness."[135] Thompson further quotes Ramsay in the following words:

> Luke is an historian of the first rank; not merely are his statements of fact trustworthy; he is possessed of the true historic sense; he fixes his mind on the idea and plan that rules in the evolution of history, and proportions the scale of his treatment of the importance of each incident. He seizes the important and critical events and shows their true nature at greater length, while he touches lightly or omits entirely much that was valueless for his purpose. In short, this author should be placed along with the very greatest of historians.[136]

It is interesting to put this statement alongside earlier acknowledgments (quoted by Thompson) where Ramsay makes it clear that in earlier years the "ingenuity and apparent completeness of the Tubingen theory . . . at one time quite convinced me."[137] Scholars from the German University at Tubingen had been prominent in their attacks against the authenticity of Luke, especially as a writer who claimed to belong to the first century A.D. Ramsay valiantly opposed those views, showing from the evidence of his own archaeological researches how fallacious they were.

Recovered Papyri Documents

The evidences for the accuracy of the New Testament can be considered in various other ways, but we shall confine ourselves to the evidences from papyrus finds. From 1875 to 1895 great quantities of papyrus documents were found in the Fayum province of Egypt, and they dated to the Roman epoch. The English investigators A. S. Hunt, B. P. Grenfell, and J. Hogarth were especially important in this work, but they were joined by German, French, and Italian investigators who also made significant discoveries. [138]

One of the most important findings in the Fayum region was by Grenfell and Hunt at Tebtunis when they uncovered a large number of mummified crocodiles. These were found to contain great quantities of papyrus that had come from the wastepaper containers of the priests before, during, and after New Testament times. Other findings soon followed, and before long it was established that these documents were basically relating to the everyday affairs of the "common" people of New Testament times. [139]

We elaborate these extensively in *New Light on the Gospels* and *New Light on New Testament Letters,* but at this stage we will simply give a few examples from these remarkable findings, especially as they relate to the life and times of Jesus.

In Luke 2:1–7, the enrollment (census) at Bethlehem is recorded. Scholars had questioned the accuracy of this narrative on four counts:

1. That a census took place in the reign of Herod, at the decree of Caesar Augustus;
2. That everyone had to return to his ancestral home;
3. That everyone in the Roman Empire was involved; and
4. That Quirinius was then Governor of Syria.

The papyrus documents recovered by Grenfell and Hunt showed that there was a fourteen-year census cycle instituted by Augustus, and that "the papyri are quite consistent with Luke's statement that this was the first enrollment."[140] They produced other documents that make it clear that the census was according to households and that those people out of their original districts were expected to return to their own homes, to cooperate with the enrollment. Grenfell and Hunt quote various documents to show that this was indeed the practice, just as Luke had made clear.

The fourth point of criticism challenged the Bible's claim that Quirinius was governor of Syria at the time. He was governor at the time of the census fourteen years later, in A.D. 6, but, it turns out that he was also a high official in central Asia Minor in 8 B.C., actually being in charge of the Army in Syria. It appears that he was able to repulse a local uprising that probably delayed the implementation of the poll tax in Syria for some time.

Various new sayings supposedly originating from Jesus were found in the papyrus fragments, and there were also new "gospels" and "epistles." The study of these fairly quickly shows how different they are from the accepted Gospels and Epistles in the New Testament. Fantasy and magic are associated with the boyhood of Jesus, and, in the supposed teachings of Jesus and of the apostles, Gnostic heresies are very evident. Such religious systems alloyed Christianity with Greek philosophy, asceticism, etc. Gnostic teaching included dangerous doctrinal departures. One example is that matter is inherently evil and that Christ's manhood involved a series of angelic mediations to overcome this problem. In contrast, the Bible teaches that He became flesh and dwelt among us, and in Him dwells all the fullness of the Godhead bodily (John 1:14; Col. 2:9).[141]

The more we study these ancient writings from Oxyrhynchus and other parts of Egypt, the more we are convinced that they are not in the same category as the canonical Gospels and Epistles. (The canon refers to the Books of the Old and New Testaments which have been traditionally accepted as the Word of God.)

Through the contrast they offer, these other documents help to vindicate the authenticity of the canonical writings.

Dean Farrar wrote long ago:

> The Four Gospels superseded all others and won their way into universal acceptance by their intrinsic value and authority. After "so many salutary losses"* we still possess a rich collection of Apocryphal Gospels, and, if they serve no other good purpose, they have this value, that they prove for us undoubtedly the unique and transcendent superiority of the sacred records. These bear the stamp of absolute truthfulness, all the more decisively when placed in contrast with writings which show signs of willful falsity. We escape from their "lying magic" to find support and help in the genuine Gospels. "And here we take refuge with the greater confidence because the ruins which lie around the ancient archives of the Church look like a guarantee of the enduring strength and greatness of those archives themselves." [142]

That comment was written nearly a century ago, and it is just as true today as when it was first written. No other "gospel" or so-called apostolic epistle has within it the "intrinsic value and authority" of the authentic New Testament writings.

New Testament Words

The documents from the embalmed crocodiles and from other recovered repositories threw a great deal of light on New Testament words. We elaborate these at great length in the two books referred to above *(New Light on the Gospels* and *New Light on New Testament Letters)*. Following are a few examples of words and incidents on which light has been thrown from the papyri.

In Matthew 25:19 the parable of the talents is recorded, and there we read of an absent lord who returned and "made a reckoning with his servants." Until the Egyptian findings, the expression "made a reckoning" was known only in the New Testament,

---

Multi conati sunt scribere Evangelia, sed non omnes recepti ("There are many who have tried to write gospels, but not all have been accepted"), Origen wrote at the beginning of the third century. This quotation indicates his knowledge of spurious "gospels" of that time.

but now it turns up in a papyrus document from Oxyrhynchus, and in fact the same expression is known in two other writings from other parts of Egypt. There are many examples like this—the discovery of everyday words, previously unknown outside the Bible, now demonstrating that the New Testament documents were authentic productions of those times.

It is somewhat surprising to know that even the word *daily* in the prayer "give us this day our daily bread" (Matt. 6:4) was unknown outside the New Testament.[143] It now turns up in the record of a house-

One of the papyri found at Oxyrhynchus in Egypt with some of the "new" sayings of Jesus. Many of these papyri have demonstrated that linguistically the New Testament documents were authentic productions of those times.

keeper's account in a reference to "a daily allowance of food." Even the common word *rain* (Greek *broche*) in the story about a man who built his house on the sand was unknown outside the New Testament. Once again, it turns up in the papyrus from Oxyrhynchus, in a document dealing with a contract for land that includes a reference to an inundation, dating to A.D. 88–89. The contracts are based on a four-year lease, with the proviso that in that time there were to be four inundations (which bring fertile blankets of sediment). Other lease documents make it clear that, in such agreements, any year that the inundation did not take place was not regarded as a year for the purposes of the contract.

The Greek word *hamatizo* ("I clothe") was known only in biblical writings, such as Mark 5:15, where the man previously possessed by a legion of demons was now seated, *clothed* and in his right mind. It seems strange that scholars only a century ago thought this was a word virtually invented for biblical purposes. These and many other similar finds have long ago convinced scholars to know that the New Testament was written in koine ("shared" or "common") Greek, the language of the ordinary people.

The papyrus has stories that in some ways are quite similar to those Jesus told, one especially interesting example being that of the Good Samaritan. The papyrus record tells of two pig merchants who were returning home when "certain malefactors came upon us between Polydeucia and Theadelphia, binding us and also the guard of the tower, and assaulted us with very many strikes, and wounded Pasion, and robbed us of one pig, and carried off Pasion's coat. . . ."[144]

This document dates to A.D. 71, and it has long ago been pointed out that if it had dated to before the Gospels were written, many scholars would have insisted that the story of the Good Samaritan was borrowed from this source. The fact is, the papyrus documents simply show that Jesus' story was based on the kind of occurrence that was probably all too familiar to his hearers.

Who would have thought that even Jesus' statements about five sparrows being sold for two farthings

(Luke 12:6) and two sparrows for a farthing (Matt. 10:29) would have light thrown on them from archaeology? An edict known as the maximum tariff comes from the time of the Roman emperor Diocletian, and it lays down the highest price at which various items can be sold, including four sparrows. Sparrows were the cheapest of all birds used for food—even cheaper than starlings. Jesus was talking about actual conditions of buying and selling, and apparently for quantity buying there was a discount price incentive!

Yet another word that was supposedly unknown was *allogenes,* which literally means "of another race," or "foreigner." It is used in the story of the healing of the ten lepers (Luke 17:18). Jesus said, "There are not found that returned to give glory to God, save this stranger." We now know that the word simply means "foreigner," and it was used in New Testament times, just as the New Testament itself makes clear.

Those who know the facts now recognize that the New Testament must be accepted as a remarkably accurate source book for those times, as evidenced by its use of words that characterized the days when Jesus walked the streets of Jerusalem and traversed the plains of Galilee.

Hebrew Still in Use

Even the statement about the inscription over the cross of Jesus is seen in a new light since the findings of the Dead Sea Scrolls. It was previously contended by some scholars that in Jesus' time the use of Hebrew had entirely given way to its sister tongue, Aramaic. Thus, New Testament references to its use were suspect. In John 19:20 we read that the inscription was written in three languages—Hebrew, Latin, and Greek. At Murabba'at, evidence was found to show that Hebrew was still a living language, not only for the priests, but also for ordinary people. One letter, from the leader of the Second Jewish Revolt (Simon Bar Kochba) to the local commander at Murabba'at, gave instructions that anybody seeking to surrender should be killed; this letter was written in Hebrew. Thus when we read of the Hebrew inscription over the cross, or about a pool having five porches that was called "Bethesda" in

Hebrew, or about the "pavement" that was "Gabbatha" in Hebrew, or about "the place of the skull" being "Golgotha" in Hebrew, it now seems that we are well grounded in relying on these reports.

These findings indicate that even in apparently insignificant details the Bible is capable of being taken as remarkably accurate. Its historical perspectives may not be those of Western historians of the twentieth century A.D., but its history is accurate history, genuinely set against the backgrounds claimed for it. It can be subjected to the closest scrutiny so long as there is legitimate recognition of the Eastern style of the book, the use of figurative language, and the literary style of those who penned the records under the guidance of the Holy Spirit of God.

The same sort of findings continue on into the Epistles. We find that the word *castaway,* used by Paul in writing to the Corinthian Christians, is also used in the sense of a vessel that has been cracked and is no longer useful for its original purpose—as when a water vessel is cracked. It cannot be used for water, but it can be put on the shelf as a container for household objects. So Paul was warning the Christians to be sure that they were not "put on the shelf," unable to fulfill the original purposes of God for their lives. The word used by Paul in that context in 1 Corinthians 9:27 is actually *adokimos* ("unapproved," "castaway," "put to one side," no longer suitable for its original purpose).

Another interesting word is *prographo* ("set forth"), a term known in various papyrus records. One case is where a father declares that he will no longer be responsible for the debts of his son because he has squandered a great deal in "riotous living," reminding us of the story of the Prodigal Son (Luke 15). The man did more than make the declaration in writing, for he had a notice posted—"placarded." The apostle Paul uses the same word in Galatians 3:1, referring to the fact that the crucifixion of Christ was not carried out in secret. It was as though Jesus was *placarded.* He was publicly displayed on the cross as though He were a criminal, and so placarded before the world.

Possibly the best known of these words is the reference in Hebrews 11:1, "Now faith is the *substance* of

things hoped for, the evidence of things not seen."
This word *hypostasis* is used in various places in the
papyrus and is related to a person's right to claim a
property; it is virtually referring to the "title deeds" of
the property. The word implies the idea of a written
undertaking with regard to property, with documents
having been properly drawn up and deposited with the
legal authorities. Thus they were the basis of ownership.

So in the area of faith, the writer of Hebrews is
telling us that though we cannot physically or mate-
rially grasp our spiritual possessions, by faith we can
claim them. The title deeds are ours.

chapter thirteen

A Concluding Survey

In summary, the evidence from archaeology has been seen to assure us repeatedly of the Bible's authenticity in terms of dating, authorship, and background. This fact, together with the anticipation of new finds, such as the Ebla tablets, warrant confidence concerning as-yet-unresolved difficulties. Archaeology has given immeasurable support to the integrity of the Bible.

Archaeological finds have consistently supported the narrative of Genesis, with recent material even lending greater support to Genesis 1–11. They have validated the history of the Hebrew people as recorded in the Old Testament and explained many biblical words, incidents, and customs that were previously obscure, setting them in a fuller context of world events and history.

The Dead Sea Scrolls, particularly those found at Qumran, have provided older Hebrew texts, further validating the strength of our manuscript evidence. Similarities tie both the New Testament and the Qumran community to Judean culture. Documents—some

123

found relatively recently in mummified crocodiles—
have shown New Testament accuracy in the once
widely doubted details of daily life, and the integrity of
the canon by contrast.

One other important conclusion is that archaeology
constantly assures us that Bible prophecies were
genuinely set against the backgrounds claimed for
them. The serious investigator has every reason for
great confidence in the reliability of both Old and New
Testament Scriptures.

This is not to say all problems have been resolved,
for some do remain. Difficulties are at times pointed
out when parallel records in different parts of the Bible
are compared. Although many similar problems have
been resolved, it may be that for others we simply do
not have all the relevant imformation and that we must
wait for further light from archaeology or another
discipline.

There are other types of problems also. A particular
happening or incident might be reported in two or more
accounts, which at first sight seem to be at variance.
However, on closer examination, it is consistently
found that the two accounts are complementary rather
than in opposition to each other. A good example is the
account of the creation of man in Genesis 2; it supple-
ments the record of Genesis 1 where the creation of all
things, and not just that of man, is described.

**Significant
Finds Continue**

Where does the story end? One need only consult the
current journals dealing with archaeology in various
lands associated with the Bible to find there is a continuing flow. We have earlier referred to the extraordinary find in September 1975 of the ancient site of Ebla,
now a tell some thirty miles south of Aleppo in Syria. It
is somewhat representative of the present course and
status of biblical archaeology that the find, which may
turn out to be the most spectacular find of our century,
is also the most recent. It will take years for scholars to
translate the approximately seventeen thousand clay
tablets unearthed at Tell Mardikh. What's more, we
have not only their secrets to look forward to, but also
an extremely early guide to the Canaanite language as
well. As mentioned in chapter 2, even at this early date

in the translation of these tablets, names heretofore unknown outside the Bible—names such as Ab-ra-mu (Abraham), Da-'u-dum (David), and Is-ra-ilu (Israel) —have been found and cities have been identified as having existed centuries earlier than was otherwise known. In some cases, such as with Jerusalem, a full millennium of history has been added. When the Italian archaeologists release fuller details of these findings to the world, it is almost certain that a great amount of new information will be added to the knowledge of Bible backgrounds.

It is true, of course, that the historical reliability of the Bible does not "prove" the factual nature of its miracles or its spiritual truths. Those are not demonstrable by proofs of a "material" nature. However, the historical material—seen through archaeology to be of remarkable integrity—is penned by the same men who witnessed and recorded the miracles and elaborated on spiritual realities. It is reasonable to believe that they would be as reliable in those areas as they are in the areas now subject to investigation by archaeology.

Another point not often made is that archaeology has supported the Bible's integrity by what it has *not* found. It is doubtful if there is a single idol of Yahweh (Jehovah) recovered from a Hebrew site, though many Canaanite Baal figures have been found. The prohibition against making an image of Yahweh was so deeply ingrained in the people that even a backsliding Israelite would not make such an image. Such a person would instead adopt Baalism or some other false worship.

In the literature recovered from Israel's neighbors, archaeologists have never found the injunctions of the Ten Commandments, the concept of holiness linked with monotheism, or the life-centered ethical and spiritual challenges such as are found in the writings of Israel's prophets.

The marks of the Bible's high integrity and superhuman foresight and wisdom are impressive when seen together with its claim that "holy men of God spoke as they were inspired by God's Holy Spirit" (2 Peter 1:21). The Bible is also a human book, penned by ordinary mortals; the Old Testament is a national history of Israel, researched and written by representatives of that nation; the New Testament is a product of its times, yet transcends its times as it presents the timeless Son of God who came to die on a cross for humanity's sin, and then to rise again.

It is the studied conviction of this writer that the Bible is not only the ancient world's most reliable history textbook; it is God's revelation of Himself in Jesus Christ.

Response

R. K. HARRISON   The factual and historical reliability of Scripture has been a matter of contention for a good many centuries. Some of the earliest attacks against Christianity denied the resurrection of Jesus as a factual event, while others rejected His messianic mission as depicted in the Scriptures. Certain groups dismissed the Old Testament in part or as a whole and cast doubt on matters such as the Mosaic authorship of the Pentateuch, the predictive element in the prophetic tradition, and the general authority of the Old Testament Scriptures. Nineteenth-century European rationalism went considerably further in some respects, dismissing outright as myth or legend many of the historical personages and events in the Old Testament narratives, assigning late dates to early elements of the Hebrew historical and religious tradition, and denigrating the concepts of biblical inspiration and authority.

It is now widely admitted that these postulates were developed when nineteenth-century theories of biological evolution were being widely proclaimed — theories that have undergone sobering modification in the light of subsequent scientific discoveries. In the same way, many of the extreme positions adopted by literary critics of the Bible have been challenged and refuted by adducing evidence recovered as the result of archaeological discoveries in the Near East.

It is to such objective data that Dr. Wilson addresses himself in his bid to demonstrate the historical credibility and accuracy of Scripture. Having been Director of the Australian Institute of Archaeology, he is eminently qualified for this task. He introduces the reader to biblical archaeology as a discipline, and is careful to point out that archaeology is not meant to prove the "truth" of the Bible, if only because metaphysical truth cannot be demonstrated by purely physical means. Relevant archaeological discoveries are of service by providing a cultural and historical background against which the biblical narrative can be examined.

Wilson surveys the history of the biblical period stage by stage, with constant reference to the relevant objective evidence furnished by archaeological discoveries. He sets the early chapters of Genesis firmly
against a Mesopotamian cultural background and pre-

sents an excellent case for considering the bulk of Genesis to have been written originally on clay tablets. He adduces convincing evidence in support of the Patriarchal and Joseph traditions, and shows how Hittite vassal treaties of the second millennium B.C. formed the pattern for God's covenant with Israel in the time of Moses.

The author confronts squarely such problems as the date of the Exodus and the settlement of Palestine by the Israelites and indicates the way in which archaeological excavations have extended our knowledge of the kingdom period, the exile, and the resettlement of Palestine. This information is presented against a background of first-hand knowledge of many of the sites discussed. Although Wilson makes a point of being fair to the various schools of interpretation of data, since differences of opinion do exist in the understanding of the nature and role of certain artifacts, he does not lose sight of the fact that there is a substantial measure of agreement in important areas of ancient Israelite history and culture.

The introduction to the Dead Sea Scrolls is rather brief, but serves nevertheless to link the intertestamental period with the ministry of Jesus, and prepares the reader for an important section on New Testament archaeology. A little more archaeological background to the ministry of Jesus would have enriched this section without enlarging it unduly. However, Wilson shows the authentic nature of the historical, cultural, and linguistic background depicted in the Gospels and other New Testament writings, and makes it abundantly clear that the accounts of early Christianity can be taken as authentic and reliable records.

This book stresses that, whatever the strengths or weaknesses of the interpretation of relevant archaeological data at any given point, the biblical records themselves were the product of a genuine human culture and were compiled and transmitted by responsible and competent individuals. God has used man's skill in this way to preserve a written record of His revelation and His salvation in Christ, and Wilson demonstrates clearly that these literary sources are indeed authentic and reliable both for history and faith.

References

[1] G. E. Wright, *Biblical Archaeology,* 7th ed. abridged (Philadelphia: Westminster, 1974), p. 10.

[2] J. A. Thompson, *The Bible and Archaeology* (Grand Rapids: Eerdmans, 1975), pp. 3–10.

[3] Merrill F. Unger, *Archaeology and the Old Testament* (Grand Rapids: Zondervan, 1954), pp. 9–25.

[4] J. B. Pritchard, *The Ancient Near Eastern Text* (Princeton: Princeton University Press, 1955), pp. 376–78.

[5] Ibid., p. 320.

[6] Ibid., p. 281.

[7] D. Whiton Thomas, *Documents from Old Testament Times* (New York: Society for Old Testament Study, 1958), pp. 204–8.

[8] Pritchard, *Ancient Text,* p. 322.

[9] Leo Deuel, *Testaments of Time* (New York: Alfred A. Knopf, 1966), pp. 133–89.

[10] J. B. Pritchard, "The Water System at Gibeon," in *Biblical Archaeologist* 39, no. 4 (December 1956): 66–75.

[11] Clifford Wilson, *That Incredible Book the Bible* (Chicago: Moody, 1973; also in paperback edition by the same publisher, 1975, pages may vary), pp. 13–39.

[12] Samuel H. Hook, *Middle Eastern Mythology* (New York: Penguin, Pelican Books, 1963), p. 114.

[13] Wilson, *That Incredible Book,* pp. 14–20.

[14] K. A. Kitchen, *Ancient Orient and the Old Testament* (Chicago: InterVarsity, 1966), pp. 88–90.

[15] Wilson, *That Incredible Book,* pp. 17–18.

[16] A. R. Millard, "A New Babylonian 'Genesis' Story," in *Tyndale Bulletin* 18 (1967): 17–18.

[17]Kitchen, *Ancient Orient*, p. 89.

[18]P. J. Wiseman, *New Discoveries in Babylonia about Genesis* (London: Marshall, Morgan and Scott, 1958), pp. 47–48.

[19]Bjorksten Research Foundation, *Twelve-Year Report (Nov. 1, 1964 to Oct. 31, 1976) of the Studies on Aging* (Madison: Bjorksten Research Foundation, 1976), pp. 1–2.

[20]Clifford Wilson, *In the Beginning God* (Grand Rapids: Baker, 1975), pp. 103–6.

[21]Ibid., pp. 41ff., 120–21.

[22]Ibid., pp. 103–6.

[23]W. F. Albright, *Recent Discoveries in Bible Lands* (New York: Funk and Wagnalls, 1955), pp. 70ff.

[24]Wilson, *In the Beginning God*, pp. 134–38.

[25]W. F. Albright, *Yahweh and the Gods of Canaan, An Historical Analysis of Two Contrasting Faiths* (New York: Doubleday, 1968), p. 87.

[26]E. A. Speiser, *Anchor Bible: Genesis* (Garden City: Doubleday, 1964), pp. 74–76.

[27]S. N. Kramer, "The Babel of Tongues—A Sumerian Version," in *Journal of the American Oriental Society* 88 (March 1968): 108–11.

[28]O. R. Gurney, *Enmerkar and the Lord of Aratta*, University Museum Monograph (n.p.: S. N. Kramer Publisher, 1952).

[29]Kramer, "Babel of Tongues," pp. 108–11.

[30]Giovanni Pettinato, "The Royal Archives of Tell Mardikh-Ebla," in *Biblical Archaeologist* 39, no. 2 (May 1976): 44–52.

[31]*Los Angeles Times*, 7 June 1976.

[32]R. K. Harrison, *Old Testament Times* (Grand Rapids: Eerdmans, 1970), pp. 80–81.

[33]Pritchard, *Ancient Text*, pp. 159–63.

[34]Ibid., pp. 159ff.

[35]Pettinato, "Royal Archives," pp. 44–52.

[36]Thompson, *The Bible and Archaeology*, pp. 27–30.

[37]Andre Parrot, *Mari, Une Ville Perdue . . .* Editions "Je Sers" (Paris: Societe Commerciale d'Edition et de Librarrie, 1945).

[38]Thompson, *Bible and Archaeology*, p. 17.

[39]W. F. Albright, *Archaeology, Historical Analogy and Early Biblical Tradition* (Baton Rouge: Louisiana State University Press, 1966), pp. 28ff.; Nelson Glueck, *Annual of the American Schools of Oriental Research,* vols. 4,15–19,25–28; idem, *The Other Side of the Jordan* (New Haven: American Schools of Oriental Research, 1940).

[40]Edward Chiera, *They Wrote on Clay,* ed. George G. Cameron (Chicago: University of Chicago Press, 1938).

[41]W. F. Albright, *From Stone-Age to Christianity* (Baltimore: Johns Hopkins Press, 1957), p. 183.

[42]Manfred R. Lehman, "Abraham's Purchase of Machpelah and Hittite Law," in *Bulletin of the American Schools of Oriental Research,* no. 129 (February 1953), pp. 15–18.

[43]O. R. Gurney, *The Hittites* (London: Penguin, Pelican Books, 1955), pp. 15ff.

[44]David N. Freedman in public lecture at the University of Michigan, November 9, 1976.

[45]Thompson, *Bible and Archaeology,* pp. 25–36.

[46]Edwin M. Yamauchi, *The Stones and the Scriptures* (New York: Lippincott, 1972), pp. 36–46.

[47]Thompson, *Bible and Archaeology,* p. 40.

[48]J. Vergote, *Joseph in Egypt* (Lauvane: Publications Universitaires, 1959).

[49]Thompson, *Bible and Archaeology,* p. 45.

[50]John A. Wilson, *The Culture of Ancient Egypt* (Chicago: Phoenix Books, 1965), pp. 257–58.

[51]Thompson, *Bible and Archaeology,* pp. 44–45.

[52]Jack Finegan, *Light From the Ancient Past* (Princeton: Princeton University Press, 1964), p. 88.

[53]G. Ernest Wright, *Biblical Archaeology* (Philadelphia: Westminster, 1963), p. 53.

[54]Unger, *Archaeology and the Old Testament,* pp. 140–52; Thompson, *Bible and Archaeology.*

[55]John Garstang, *Joshua–Judges* (London: Constable, 1931), pp. 143ff.

[56]Kitchen, *Ancient Orient,* pp. 147–48.

[57]W. F. Albright, "Archaeological Discovery and the Scriptures," in *Christianity Today* 12, no. 19 (21 June 1968): 4.

[58]George E. Mendenhall, "Biblical History in Transition," *The Bible and the Ancient Near East,* ed. G. Ernest Wright (Garden City: Doubleday, Anchor Books, 1965), pp. 36ff.

[59]Ibid., p. 42.

[60]Kitchen, *Ancient Orient,* p. 91.

[61]Ibid., pp. 98–99.

[62]G. Ernest Wright, "Biblical Archaeology Today," *New Directions in Biblical Archaeology,* ed. Freedman and Greenfield (New York: Doubleday, 1971), p. 173.

[63]Ibid., p. 15.

[64]Unger, *Archaeology and the Old Testament,* p. 160.

[65]Edwin R. Thiele, *The Mysterious Numbers of the Hebrew Kings,* rev. ed. (Grand Rapids: Eerdmans, 1965).

[66]Kitchen, *Ancient Orient,* p. 70.

[67]John and J. B. E. Garstang, *The Story of Jericho* (London: Marshall, Morgan and Scott, 1948), pp. 37–38.

[68]W. F. Albright, "Researches of the School in Western Judaea," in *Bulletin of the American Schools of Oriental Research,* no. 15 (October 1924), pp. 7–8.

[69]Wilson, *That Incredible Book,* p. 81.

[70]Ibid., pp. 82–86.

[71]Wright, "Biblical Archaeology Today," p. 81.

[72]C. F. Pfeiffer, ed., *The Biblical World* (Grand Rapids: Baker, 1966), p. 448.

[73]W. F. Albright, *Archaeology of Palestine* (Baltimore: Penguin Books, 1963), p. 115.

[74]B. Maisler, "The Excavation of Tell Qasile," in *Biblical Archaeologist* 14, no. 2 (May 1951): 44.

[75]Thompson, *Bible and Archaeology,* p. 81.

[76]Albright, *Archaeology of Palestine,* pp. 120–22; Paul W. Lapp, "Tell el-Ful," in *Biblical Archaeologist* 28, no. 1 (February 1965): 2–10.

[77]Pfeiffer, *Biblical World,* p. 92.

[78]A. Rowe, *Beth-shan: Four Canaanite Temples* (Philadelphia: University of Pennsylvania Press, 1940), pp. 23, 31.

[79]H. L. Ginsberg, "A Ugaritic Parallel to II Samuel 1:21," *Journal of Biblical Literature* 57 (1938): 209–13.

[80]W. F. Albright, "The Old Testament and Archaeology," in *Old Testament Commentary,* ed. H. C. Alleman and E. G. Flack (Philadelphia: Muhlenberg, 1954), p. 149.

[81]Kathleen Kenyon, *Royal Cities of the Old Testament* (New York: Schocken, 1971), pp. 24–27.

[82]W. F. Albright, *Archaeology and the Religion of Israel* (New York: Doubleday, Anchor Books, 1969), pp. 125–27.

[83]W. F. Albright, *History, Archaeology, and Christian Humanism* (New York: McGraw-Hill, 1964), pp. 34–35.

[84]Wilson, *That Incredible Book*, p. 93.

[85]Thompson, *Bible and Archaeology*, p. 101.

[86]Nelson Glueck, *The River Jordan* (Philadelphia: Westminster, 1946), p. 146; idem, *The Other Side of the Jordan* (New Haven: American Schools of Oriental Research, 1940), pp. 50ff.; idem, "Ezion-geber," in *Biblical Archaeologist* 28, no. 3 (September 1965): 70–87.

[87]Pfeiffer, *Biblical World*, p. 290.

[88]Yigael Yadin, "Temple Scroll" in *American Schools of Oriental Research Newsletter* no. 7 (13 November 1967): 8.

[89]Yigael Yadin, "An Inscribed South-Arabian Clay Stamp from Bethal?" in *Bulletin of the American Schools of Oriental Research,* no. 196 (December 1969): 38.

[90]Wendell Phillips, *Qataban and Sheba* (New York: Harcourt, Brace, 1955), pp. 279–80.

[91]Yohanan Aharoni, "Forerunners in the Limes: Iron Age Fortresses on the Negev," in *Israel Exploration Journal* 17, no. 1 (1967): 1.

[92]Albright, *Archaeology of Palestine*, p. 123.

[93]B. Mazar, "The Campaign of Pharaoh Shishak to Palestine," in *Vetus Testamentum* 4 (1957): 59.

[94]D. D. Luckenbill, *Ancient Records of Assyria and Babylonia*, vols. 1 and 2 (Chicago: University of Chicago Press, 1926–27; reprint ed., Westport, Conn.: Greenwood, 1969); A. Olmstead, *History of Assyria* (New York: Scribner, 1923); H. W. F. Saggs, *Everyday Life in Babylonia and Assyria* (London: Putnam, 1965).

[95]Pfeiffer, *Biblical World*, pp. 137–38.

[96]Finegan, *Light from Past*, p. 217.

[97]Thompson, *Bible and Archaeology,* pp. 111–13.

[98]Ibid., p. 129.

[99]Pritchard, *Ancient Text*, p. 320.

[100]Ibid., pp. 278–79.

[101] Austen Layard, *Nineveh and Its Remains* (New York: Praegar, 1849), 1:282.

[102] Pritchard, *Ancient Text,* pp. 283ff.

[103] Ibid. p. 286.

[104] Albright, "Old Testament and Archaeology," pp. 161ff.; Millar Burrows, *What Mean These Stones?* (New Haven: American Schools of Oriental Research, 1941), pp. 43ff.

[105] Pritchard, *Ancient Text,* pp. 284ff.

[106] Ibid., p. 288.

[107] D. D. Luckenbill, *The Annals of Sennacherib* (Chicago: University of Chicago Press, 1924), p. 24.

[108] Pritchard, *Ancient Text,* pp. 288ff.

[109] Luckenbill, *Ancient Records,* vol. 2, sec. 501–2, pp. 200–201.

[110] Ibid., sec. 795, p. 304.

[111] Pritchard, *Ancient Text,* p. 208.

[112] W. F. Albright, *The Biblical Period from Abraham to Ezra* (New York: Harper and Row, 1963), pp. 85–86, 95.

[113] Pritchard, *Ancient Text,* pp. 305ff.; Finegan, *Light from Past,* pp. 189ff.

[114] R. H. Pfeiffer, *Old Testament Introduction* (New York: Harper and Brothers, 1944), pp. 758–59.

[115] Pritchard, *Ancient Text,* pp. 315ff.

[116] W. F. Albright, "The Bible after Twenty Years of Archaeology—1932–1952," in *Religion in Life* 21, no. 4 (1952; also reprinted separately, Pittsburg: Biblical Colloquium, 1954): 546–47.

[117] A. Olmstead, *The History of the Persian Empire* (Chicago: University of Chicago Press, 1948), p. 295.

[118] F. M. Cross, "Geshem the Arab, Enemy of Nehemiah," in *Biblical Archaeologist* 18, no. 2 (May 1955): 47; William J. Dumbrell, "The Tell El-Maskhuta Bowls and the 'Kingdom' of Qedar in the Persian Period," in *Bulletin of the American Schools of Oriental Research,* no. 203 (October 1971), pp. 33–34.

[119] F. M. Cross, "The Discovery of the Samaria Papyri," in *Biblical Archaeologist* 26, no. 4 (December 1963): 110–21.

[120] Thiele, *Mysterious Numbers,* p. 201.

[121] Ibid.

[122]Yadin, "Temple Scroll."

[123]F. F. Bruce, *The Teacher of Righteousness in the Qumran Texts* (London: Tyndale, 1957), p. 77; T. H. Gaster, *The Dead Sea Scriptures* (New York: Doubleday, 1957), p. 5.

[124]Thompson, *Bible and Archaeology,* pp. 262ff.

[125]Wilson, *That Incredible Book,* pp. 160–62.

[126]W. S. LaSor, *The Dead Sea Scrolls and the Christian Faith* (Chicago: Moody, 1976), p. 153.

[127]Finegan, *Light from Past,* pp. 272ff.

[128]Ibid., pp. 269,278.

[129]Wilson, *That Incredible Book,* pp. 164–70.

[130]LaSor, *Scrolls and Faith,* pp. 207ff.

[131]A. Dupont-Sommer, *The Jewish Sect of Qumran and the Essenes,* trans. R. D. Barnett (London: Vallentine, Mitchell, 1954), pp. 51–52 (quoted by LaSor, *Scrolls and Faith,* p. 167).

[132]LaSor, *Scrolls and Faith,* pp. 167ff.

[133]Sir William Ramsay, *St. Paul the Traveller and the Roman Citizen* (Grand Rapids: Baker, 1960), pp. 7–8.

[134]J. A. Thompson, *Luke the Historian* (Melbourne: Australian Institute of Archaeology, 1954), p. 14.

[135]Ibid., p. 29.

[136]Ibid.

[137]Ibid., p. 30.

[138]Clifford Wilson, *New Light on the Gospels* (London: Lakeland, 1970), pp. 14ff.

[139]B. P. Grenfell and A. S. Hunt, *The Oxyrhynchus Papyri,* parts 2 and 4 (London: Oxford University Press, 1899 and 1904).

[140]Ibid., part 2, pp. 211ff.

[141]Wilson, *New Light,* pp. 39ff.,45,47,49ff.

[142]F. W. Farrar, *The Messages of the Books* (London: Macmillan, 1884), p. 27.

[143]Wilson, *New Light,* p. 75.

[144]Ibid., p. 88.

For Further Reading

Albright, William F. **Archeology and the Religion of Israel.** Garden City: Doubleday and Co., Inc., 1969.

Albright shows the distinctiveness of the Hebrew view of the world and religion in contradistinction to surrounding nature myths.

Albright, William F. **From the Stone Age to Christianity, Monotheism and the Historical Process.** Garden City: Anchor Books, Doubleday and Co., Inc., 1957.

Albright centers on the question of historical process and traces monotheism from the Stone Age to the time of Christ. He argues that monotheism, rooted in the ancient Near East, is the key to the history of human civilization in the West.

Bruce, F. F. **New Testament Documents: Are They Reliable?** Grand Rapids: Eerdmans, 1960.

Bruce gives an articulate defense of the historical accuracy of the New Testament manuscripts and the reliability of their transmission down through the centuries.

Gardiner, Alan. **Egypt of the Pharaohs: An Introduction.** New York: Oxford University Press, 1961. Oxford Paperbacks, 1964.

A classic introduction to Egyptology—the study of ancient Egypt dealing with the foundations and nature of Egyptian history, language and writing, and Egyptian history from the earliest times to the conquest of Alexander the Great in 332 B.C.

Harrison, R. K. **Introduction to the Old Testament.**
Grand Rapids: Eerdmans, 1969.

*A survey of critical problems related to Old Testament
books, dealing with critical reconstruction, the Well-
hausen hypothesis, and giving the date, historical circumstances, author, and archaeological background for each
book.*

Heidel, Alexander. **The Gilgamesh Epic and Old
Testament Parallels.** Chicago: University of Chicago
Press, 1958. Phoenix Books, 1963.

*A classic refutation of the theory that the Old Testament
account of the deluge was borrowed from Babylonian
sources.*

Kitchen, K. A. **Ancient Orient and Old Testament.**
Downers Grove: Inter-Varsity Press, 1966.

*Kitchen discusses the authorship of the Pentateuch, early
biblical chronology, and the date of the Exodus in light of
recent archaeological investigation in the Near East.*

Livingston, G. Herbert. **The Pentateuch in Its Cultural Environment.** Grand Rapids: Baker Book
House, 1974.

*An excellent introduction to the archaeological background
of the Pentateuch including dating methods and ancient Near
Eastern empires and their bearing on early Hebrew history.*

Pfeiffer, Charles F., ed. **The Dead Sea Scrolls and
the Bible.** Baker Studies in Biblical Archaeology.
Grand Rapids: Baker Book House, 1969.

*A helpful introduction to the discoveries at Qumran that have
shed new light on the accuracy of the transmission of the Old
Testament texts and on Christian origins.*

Ramsay, Sir William M. **The Bearing of Recent Discovery on the Trustworthiness of the New Testament.** London: Hodder, 1920.

*The author, one of the world's greatest authorities on the
geography and history of Asia Minor, determined to document the errors and found instead the evidence for the historicity of the Book of Acts.*

Thompson, John A. **The Bible and Archaeology.**
Grand Rapids: Eerdmans, 1975.

Thompson's scholarly survey is one of the best introductions to the world of Bible times available today. The revised edition includes a great deal of recent material.

Wiseman, P. J. **New Discoveries in Babylonia About Genesis.** London: Marshall, Morgan and Scott, 1958.

Studies in archaeology and Genesis concerning the authorship, origin, and composition of the book. Wiseman examines both the internal testimony of Genesis and the external evidence of archaeology.

Yamauchi, Edwin. **The Stones and the Scriptures.** Philadelphia: J. B. Lippincott Co., 1972.

An up-to-date introduction to archaeology with special reference to the assertions of the Bible's critics in light of archaeological discovery. Well indexed.

Notes